KO,

I picked this up at a local bookstore and thought it might help catch you up on the last eighteen years. I hope that when they write the next one after the next hundred years my name is mentioned somewhere alongside yours as a loyal and devoted Assistant to the Program.

Thanks for the support and encouragement on this trip. I hope we can develop a long and meaningful professional relationship.

Sincerest Thanks and Best Wishes,

Luke

P.S.
Nice story on page 104!

Tales from the

ARIZONA WILDCATS
HARDWOOD

Steve Rivera

www.SportsPublishingLLC.com

ISBN: 1-58261-616-7

Interior images provided by Collegiate Images, unless otherwise noted

Publisher: Peter L. Bannon
Senior managing editor: Susan M. Moyer
Acquisitions editor: Mike Pearson
Developmental editor: Doug Hoepker
Art director: K. Jeffrey Higgerson
Dust jacket design: Christine Mohrbacher
Project manager: Kathryn R. Holleman
Imaging: Dustin Hubbart and Christine Mohrbacher
Photo editor: Erin Linden-Levy
Vice president of sales and marketing: Kevin King
Media and promotions managers: Kelley Brown (regional),
        Randy Fouts (national), Maurey Williamson (print)

Printed in the United States of America

Sports Publishing L.L.C.
804 North Neil Street
Champaign, IL 61820

Phone: 1-877-424-2665
Fax: 217-363-2073
Web site: www.SportsPublishingLLC.com

To my best friend and wife, Lynda, who was patient with me throughout the project.

And to Cameron and Trey, two of the best boys any man would be proud to call sons.

CONTENTS

ACKNOWLEDGMENTS

Where do you start when you have a century's worth of people to thank for a project that proved to be energizing, insightful and fruitful?

This book seemed like a daunting task—retell the great memories of some of the exceptional players who had the talent to wear an Arizona uniform and the people who had the patience to coach them.

First, there was the task of locating many of the key figures. And there were plenty. Thanks to all—perhaps too many to mention—60-plus individuals who spent time with me, telling their insightful stories. There were some good times, some terrible times, but all interesting nonetheless.

Thanks to Fred W. Enke and his tremendous file of press clippings and his wealth of insight into the program's early years. Also, thanks to Bob Honea and Leo Johnson, who played through some of Arizona's first glory years of the postwar era.

Then there were the players and figures who made extra time in their lives for me to get through a daunting task. They include: Steve Kerr, Miles Simon, Jason Terry, Matt Muehlebach, Bruce Larson, Lute Olson, Richard Jefferson, Rick Anderson, Luke Walton, Justin Wessel, Mike Bibby, Bob Elliott. Jud Buechler, Harvey Mason, Bruce Fraser, Sean Rooks, Corey Williams, Reggie Geary, Joe McLean, Joseph Blair, Loren Woods, Sean Elliott, Steve Condon, Ryan Hansen, Rich Paige, Tom Duddleston, Brett Hansen, Ernie McCray, Warren Rustand, Albert Johnson, Joe Nehls, Dylan Rigdon, Sean Elliott and many, many more.

And thanks to those who had similar projects throughout the years of Arizona basketball: Abe Channin, Steve Cameron, Janet Mitchell and John Moredich. Good job to all.

And finally, thanks to media outlets: *Tucson Citizen, Arizona Daily Star, Arizona Republic,* Associated Press, United Press International, *Wall Street Journal, New York Times,* and *Los Angeles Times* for their background information.

Chapter 1

THE EARLY YEARS
1900-1945

HUMBLE BEGINNINGS

Seven years after John Naismith invented the game of basketball, the first recorded competition at the University of Arizona involved a group of students who gathered enough money to buy a ball. Their fun was shortlived.

Playing on a dirt court—and with a poorly made ball—the students' game didn't last long. The ball went flat.

THE FIRST YEAR

Hard to imagine, but it's been 100 years since UA officially started its program. Now players from all over arrive on scholarships to play for UA and coach Lute Olson. That wasn't the case in the first season, when only five students—that's all you need—lettered in 1905.

One guy was named Charlie Brown.

"Back then nobody gave a damn about the sport," said Tom Sanders, a longtime Arizona adminstrator and sports historian. "And you can assume the coaching was so rudimentary. Looking back, it was probably difficult to find people who wanted to play. It was still in the early stages of development." In fact, Arizona basketball didn't take off—relatively speaking—until the 1920s.

"It was pretty much just a glorified intramural sport," said Jon Alquist, one of the most notable UA sports historians. "Even a recreational activity more than anything."

NICE FOOTBALL TEAM

Viewing pictures of the old-time teams—Arizona in the early years—it would seem the photos were of undermanned football teams. The reason? Arizona played in old football uniforms.

"If you look closely at those early photos," Sanders said, "they've got football pants on. They didn't get real shorts (basketball shorts) until 1920 or so. Arizona just didn't have the budget for it."

MCKALE AND ROUNDBALL

It's well documented that Pop McKale didn't particularly like basketball. His sports were football and baseball. But after being named UA's athletic director in 1914, he was also named coach in all sports. He wasn't half bad, finishing with a 49-12 record duirng his seven seasons.

"I remember the time when we went on the road to play six games in six days and won them all," McKale told reporters. "Of course, there were some obstacles. When we played the New Mexico Miners, their gym was awfully cold, so they put up a stove in the southeast corner of the court. It took up about six feet of the playing court, so they just put up a fence around the stove. We ran around the stove and I guess we didn't do too badly. We beat them 64–15."

James F. "Pop" McKale, the father of Arizona Athletics, wasn't too keen on basketball despite a 49-12 record as a coach.

PIERCE ARRIVES

Pop McKale was known not to like basketball much—if at all. So in 1921 he happened on a man passing through Arizona on his way to California via Indiana hoping to make something of his life. The man was James H. Pierce, getting introduced through friends from Phoenix where Pierce briefly lived before moving to Tucson.

In the summer of 1921, McKale was looking for a basketball coach and assistant football coach, and he had heard of Pierce from his football-playing days at Indiana. Two months after meeting McKale and the school getting approval for the hire, Pierce packed up his bags and left Los Angeles, where he had been working various jobs.

"McKale and I hit it off well," Pierce wrote in his book, *The Battle of Hollywood*. "The chemistry between us was just right and we became great friends with deep respect for each other and our jobs."

Pierce, who had signed a $2,500 contract, assisted McKale in football and coached basketball in 1921-22.

"I introduced a lot of new ideas to the Arizona team and it really blossomed," Pierce wrote. "The bounce pass, for instance, startled Arizonans the first time they saw it." On one trip to play the New Mexico Military Institute, UA players were approached by their competitors to see if they were willing to bet on their team. UA players didn't have much money, at least not like the players from NMMI. UA players declined.

But Pierce didn't. He gathered his team and said he'd front the money on any bets. After doing it, Pierce realized his job was on the line if anyone back home found out. His players vowed silence.

What did Pierce just do? He bet the team's expense money. UA had to win—or else. And it did, rallying for a second-half victory.

"But that ended my career as a would-be gambler," Pierce wrote.

ME TARZAN

After his first year at Arizona, Pierce, a striking man, met a young co-ed, Lillie Belle, and a football player, Kirk LaShelle, who would eventually change his life. LaShelle's father was a stage producer in New York. The two were introduced, and soon after, Pierce got the acting bug, getting bit parts in movies.

Belle, then a girlfriend, thought Pierce was better off not being a coach, believing a lawyer would be more stable. Anything but a coach, she said. She also didn't want to be in Arizona, having grown up there. She encouraged him to resign after a 10-2 season and head West to become a full-fledged actor.

"I was offered a long-term contract with a substantial raise in pay and was assured that if my plans ever changed, I could always find a job there," Pierce wrote of the UA.

Pierce never returned, running a gamut of jobs, including being a coach again.

Years later, Pierce became known for playing Tarzan in the movies.

THE FIRST STAR

In Arizona's first two decades of play, there was no one better than Harold Tovrea, who earned four letters and was captain of the 1923 and 1924 teams. He averaged 15.8 points in 1923 and 17.3 points in 1924, scoring more than half the points many times in Arizona's games.

"He was a phenom in the sport at UA at the time," Alquist said.

In a game that established many records for the time, Tovrea scored a school-record 35 points in a 77-17 win over

New Mexico Miners. The 77 points was also a school record. He finished with 805 points, yet another school record that stood for more than 25 years.

"He was an excellent athlete," said Tom Sanders, a long-time UA administrator who helped in compiling a history of the program for the school. "He was a scratch golfer. He was also an excellent baseball player who also wanted to play foot-ball just so he could do something."

AN ASSIST FROM KNUTE ROCKNE

Arizona basketball coach Pop McKale didn't like basketball too much. And after James A. Pierce ran off to Hollywood to become Tarzan in the early 1920s, McKale sought the help of midwesterner Knute Rockne.

Rockne, of Notre Dame fame, recommended a man he had seen work basketball clinics throughout the Midwest. His name was Fred A. Enke, who had been at Louisville two years.

Upon visiting Tucson, UA administrators took him to the Wetmore pool (a big thing back then), Herring Hall, and sites around campus. One problem was UA didn't have a sizeable gym.

Enke took the job anyway.

"He came there in a Model T," said Fred W. Enke, Enke's son. "It had no windows. But it had a tent that came out of the side. My parents and I drove a couple of thousand miles to get here. It was quite a gamble."

Fred W. was just a baby back then.

"One time in a conversation we had while talking about it, I told him I didn't think he was too smart in coming, that he was taking a big chance," Fred W. said. "Arizona had been a state for just 12 years. They gave him a salary of about $1,800 (in reports Fred A. Enke said he made $3,000). It was a big move. Now I realize it."

Big indeed. En route to Tucson somewhere between Arizona and Oklahoma, the car found trouble.

"Pappy (his son's name for his dad) missed a turn and we fell into a river," Fred W. said.

"Everything we owned was in that car, and it went into the river. A car came by and four people helped pick up the car and we moved on. I guess he must have had an adventurous side to him."

BEAR DOWN OPENS

In a major move to the big time, Arizona opened up a facility that was later called Bear Down Gym in 1926 It seated about 4,000 fans. But the first day it opened there already was trouble.

"There wasn't anything to equal it in the Southwest," Enke Sr., told reporters back then. "President Marvin had decided he wanted to open the gymnasium with a big party.

"McKale was against that because he felt dancing would ruin the floor, and it really was a beautiful floor. Well, they had the party and sprinkled cornmeal on the floor so they could dance. That really made McKale angry; they had to go in there after the dance and clean up with a special cleaning fluid."

After winning two straight in Southern California, Arizona returned home to face in-state rival Arizona State on consecutive days. In the first game, the dedication game—on January 21, 1927—school officials wanted a huge turnout so they distributed 1,500 free tickets to fans.

As it turned out the crowd was unbelievable for the times. More than 3,000 fans showed up—the most to see a basketball game in the state at the time—to see the Wildcats defeat the team from Tempe, 29-18. Waldo Dicus led UA with 10 points, hitting five shots.

On this night of basketball it was announced that Button Salmon's last message to his football teammates the year before would be the school's sports slogan.

Salmon's message of "Tell the boys to 'bear down'" was unanimously passed through the school's higher-ups to become the motto. A day later, UA defeated ASU again, this time 32-25. UA eventually went 4-0 against ASU, having won the next series by big margins in Tempe. Arizona capped off what was then called "its Salt River Valley Invasion" with a four-game complete sweep, adding victories over the Mesa Jaycees and Phoenix Junior College.

The team did suffer a loss, however, just after the sweep.

SEASON ENDS

Fred Enke's second season—1926-27—proved to be an over-whelming success as UA finished the season 13-4. In fact, in its win over Whittier College, some of the team's best basketball of the season was being played. One reporter described one play as being the best all season: "Diebold ran the ball on a pass from Miller and shot it hot off the griddle to Brooksheire in the right corner who dropped in a clean side shot for the Cats."

Arizona was victorious 30-17, taking two of three games from Whittier on the season.

DROPPING LIKE FLIES

Midway through the 1928 season, Enke dealt with something that's common nowadays—grade problems. Midway through the season, Enke dismissed three players. Theodore Diebold, Neil Goodman and a player named Turner (no first name given) were dismissed because of academics.

"We found some old transcripts," said Tom Sanders, a school historian and administrator. "And some of the students were marginal students at best. Same 'ol, same 'ol."

Enke then asked Harry Butts—yes, that was his name — to return to the team after leaving in 1926. What Enke was looking for were strong reserves, something he lacked at the time because of the players' academic problems. Despite Arizona's lack of players, it went on to close the season with five consecutive victories—all coming on the road.

BUS PROBLEMS

In the mid-'30s Arizona traveled by bus, making trips through the Rocky Mountains or to the Midwest through the plains. In 1934, Arizona went through a series of bus problems going through a then-unheard-of nine-game road trip to El Paso, Oklahoma City, Indiana and Chicago, among others.

After winning just three of the nine games, UA headed home on the charter bus on a bus line called "Blue Eagle."

"We made it all right on that bus until we left St. Louis, heading for Tulsa," Enke said, back then. "The old connecting rods went through the bottom of the crankcase."

Arizona players got their belongings and started to hitch-hike to Tulsa, where they had reservations to stay the night.

Arizona got another bus and was headed to Oklahoma City when halfway through, the bus caught on fire.

How Tom Sanders heard it, the team "hooked up the exhaust to the back of the bus to get some heating inside." That was a serious mistake as asphyxiation could have occured.

"We scrambled out of the bus, got our bags out and helped put out the fire," Enke said. "We got another bus and headed back to Tucson."

UA had to hurry. They were scheduled to play Texas Tech in Tucson a couple of days later. The players slept on the bus for two nights in their rush to get back. UA fell in its next two games to Texas Tech.

"We had a bunch of dead cookies for players," Enke said. "Considering everything, they did pretty well in losing by four points (33-29) to Tech."

A day later, UA was still tired, losing again to TT 38-27. But Enke felt strong about how well his team had played and how it handled the adversity. UA won 10 straight games and 11 of 12 after that, finishing second in the Border Conference.

HE'S GOOD, REAL GOOD

Lorry DiGrazia, a two-time team captain in 1937-38, was Arizona's first three-time all-conference performer. He was also the first Wildcat to lead the team in scoring for three consecutive seasons, finishing with a career total of 611 points. In his three years with UA he was responsible for 23.7 percent of the team's total points.

"He was light years ahead of everybody," said teammate John Black. "He dribbled between his legs, could pass and shoot. He was small at 5-10, but he was faster than hell. He was the best ballplayer I ever saw with the exception of Hank Luisetti."

Cold Trip

It wasn't often Arizona traveled long distances, but in December of 1939, Arizona was ready to embark on a four-game trip to Oklahoma to play in the All-College Tournament in Oklahoma City, Oklahoma.

In Tucson there was an unusual occurrence—it was snowing as the team left. About 120 miles into the trip, UA's team bus—one that held about 12 people—spun out. It landed in a ditch. But the team was able to get back on the road, continuing to face storms throughout the trip. The bus had little to no heat in it with only a small area getting heat.

"We all fought for that seat," said John Black.

Eventually they got through to Texas where an accident occurred—again!

"We spun out and went into a ditch. All 10 of us had to push ourselves out. It was an ice storm in Amarillo, Texas. It was quite a trip."

And a winless one. UA lost all four games, starting out the season 0-6.

Basketbrawl Game

John Black loved to mix it up every now and again. And in 1940-41 he did just that in El Paso when UA played against the Miners. Back then—at least in El Paso—the teams had to go to a community shower after a game because the facilities were so inadequate.

In the shower, UA player George Jordan gave a Texas Western player the finger. The Miner player asked him what it meant.

"What do you think it means?" said Jordan, who then hit the Miner.

Jordan later was knocked down, and then Black jumped in.

"Then some guy let me have it," Black said. "All the other guys ran for help."

That was a mistake.

"They kicked the shit out of us," Black said. "They roughed us up." But all year long the two talked about getting even. They just wanted to get them in Tucson. And in came Texas Western.

"Jordan asked me if I was in or not," Black said. "Jordan wanted to get them at the beginning of the game. He started harassing them, going down the bench and they grabbed him and held him. I came up and helped him. It turned into a hell of a rhubarb."

The next night all parties involved in the fight didn't play because they were suspended.

TEXAS TECH CHILL

On a trip to east Texas to play Texas Tech, the Wildcats were in for a rude awakening and some cold weather.

To help warm the place up—not like it could be done—Texas Tech officials used a pot bellied, wood-burning stove.

"They played in that old gym and the wind would blow through there and it would be cold," Black said.

Then there was another problem. The wind would blow dirt and sand through the door's cracks and get all over the floor, making the floor almost unplayable.

"If you tried to stop, you couldn't," said Black. "I remember Fred said, 'God damn Berl (Huffman), can't you clean the floor?'

"Tech officials made matters worse by coming in and spraying the floor. All it did was make the floor sticky and muddy."

VERY GOOD TEAM

After going 9-13 in 1941-42, Arizona turned into a power in 1942-43. In fact, it was the best season ever for the Wildcats. They finished 22-2.

On the team was Marvin Borodkin, who later left to join the war after the season.

"I signed in 1942 and was called into the air force in 1943 along with 6,000 others," Borodkin said. "We thought we had a pretty good team. At least it was the biggest and the best on the court at the time."

It was a scary time in the United States, but to the players it was what life was about.

"We were concentrating on school and playing basketball and getting a better record," Borodkin said. "We all knew we were going into the service, so it didn't bother us. We had anticipated it."

UDALL MAKES MARK

Stewart Udall is mostly known for politics, but in 1939 and 1940 he was a Wildcat star, eventually becoming an all-conference pick. He left for military service after 1940 but returned six years later.

"My great days were before the war," Udall said. "I went without playing basketball—a single game—while in the service. That was unusual. But some athletes say once you develop a skill that you don't lose it."

Upon returning in 1946, he joined a pretty good team and he was, well, not like he used to be.

"I was the old man of the group," he said. "I had one year of eligibility left but was rusty. I had my shot. For one game I was the high-point man. But then all the young guys came back from the war—Fred Enke, Jr., and Link Richmond. I was the steady influence on them.

"I just wasn't as good as I had been. I could still hit the long-range shot, but ..."

Udall's biggest contribution upon his return was petitioning the school to play a tougher schedule.

What Udall eventually wanted was to start a home-and-home schedule with perennially tough Wyoming, arguably then one of the most respected schools in the west.

"(Pop) McKale didn't want it," Udall said. "I figured if we played Wyoming it would put us on the map to the big time."

McKale brushed it off.

"Marvin (Borodkin) and I were furious," Udall said. "You just couldn't talk to McKale. Enke told us it wasn't going to happen. We knew that. Marvin and I weren't kids. So we made an appointment with the president, but he was a stuffy old man. We made this pitch that it would help the school, that it would help Arizona's basketball prestige. He listened for about eight minutes."

Then they were dismissed. "He said he understood our enthusiasm and grit, but the decision had already been made to not do it.

"He then looked at us and said, 'You are here at this university to learn, not to think,'" Udall said.

As Borodkin and Udall left the office, Udall said, "Isn't that a killer?" and "We laughed all the way out."

Chapter 2

POSTWAR SUCCESS

WE'LL JOIN IN

Shortly after World War II, just a couple of weeks in fact, Fred Enke, Jr., and Lincoln Richmond had a couple of decisions to make: either stay in the military for another four years or head home to Arizona and go to school.

"We decided to come back and play for UA," said Enke, whose father was by now in his 21st year as head coach of the Wildcats.

Frankie Downs, from Miami, Arizona, was to have joined them, but a twist of fate didn't allow him to do so. The reason? Just days before they were to leave, Downs lost about $800 playing poker, Enke said.

"It was all he had, so he signed up for four more years," Enke said.

During the trip back, Enke and Richmond, buddies since the third grade, and two others decided to make a stopover at the annual Army-Navy football game in Philadelphia. Problem was they were returning in a convertible. Back then there was no heat or air conditioning in cars.

"It was snowy and cold," Enke remembered of that December weather in 1945. "Coming back we'd sit on each other and on each other's feet just to keep warm."

Finally upon returning to Tucson, Enke's mother fixed the boys some spaghetti before they headed off to join the team in San Diego.

"We weren't even in school," said Enke. "But mom had said that dad already got everything taken care of and had it worked out because all of us had intended on going to school."

And what about the uniforms?

"Pappy has the uniforms," his mom told him.

Two days after Christmas, the guys walked into a hotel, shook their new teammates hands and worked out informally before facing San Diego State.

"The practice was on the mezzanine floor of the hotel," said Marvin Borodkin. "We went through a walk-through just so we'd all know where we were supposed to go."

Arizona proceeded to win nine straight games.

"That's when we got things going," said Enke, Jr.

In that same game, Hilliard "Junior" Crum, who is from Arizona, was at the game as a fan. He was stationed in San Diego while in the navy. A month later, he too was playing for the Cats.

"We were glad they joined in," said Borodkin.

FROM R&R TO HOOPS

At the start of the 1945-46 season, Arizona was a pretty good team, going 3-3 to start the season. It had lost the two games

Fred W. Enke, son of Arizona head coach Fred A. Enke Sr., was a hometown hero who starred for UA in the postwar era.

prior to its trip to San Diego—before Enke and Richmond joined—but was still competitive.

Marvin Borodkin was already on the team after the war, having come back to Tucson for some R&R after flying bombers in China.

"I came back to the university to chat with Fred Enke, Sr.," said Borodkin, who had lettered at UA in 1942 and 1943. "Fred asked why I didn't make the trip to New Mexico and Texas."

Borodkin said he couldn't because he was still in the air force. But Coach Enke found a way to register Borodkin for 12 audited classes. Eventually, Borodkin stayed in Tucson and UA.

"That wouldn't get by today," Borodkin said. "At least that's the theory."

So he made the trip.

OLDER, WISER PLAYERS

It was no surprise that Arizona was pretty good after the war as the best players were now in their early 20s after having been in the war at least two years. Stewart Udall, Junior Crum, Enke, Jr., and Richmond were all cagey veterans by now. To be fair, however, other schools benefited from the country's GI Bill, where former military personnel went back to school to get an education. Arizona was not alone. Players were getting married. Players were smoking. They were, well, just older.

"I remember one afternoon we were getting ready to catch the train to San Francisco. We caught it about two in the afternoon, and the next morning my first son was born. I passed out cigars so we were smoking cigars on the train," recalled Crum, of the 1948-49 season when he was 24.

The Bid

When the new players joined the team, Arizona suddenly turned into a power. After winning nine straight, Arizona then was upset by Northern Arizona—one of the few loses it had was to the Lumberjacks—but then rattled off 13 straight wins, creating a buzz in the process. Arizona was now in for a post-season bid. All they had to do is hear from the NIT committee whether it was in or not, after beating West Texas in the Border Conference title game 44-37 on March 2.

Arizona got the invite through a telegram: "Wish to extend Arizona cordial invitation to compete in the National Intercollegiate Invitational basketball tournament at New York City March 14-16-18-20 ..."

Arizona accepted and headed East. It was the first time a UA team had played competitively out East since the polo team went that far in the mid-1930s.

Facing the Wildcats ... From Kentucky

The good news was that Arizona got a bid. The not-so-good news was it was to face Kentucky.

Arizona was clearly the underdog with many not knowing how good Arizona was despite its 25-4 record. Coach Enke was undeterred about the pairing against top-seed Kentucky.

En route to New York City, Arizona had stopovers in Kansas City and then Chicago.

"When we got to Kansas City we picked up the paper and found out we were going to play Kentucky," recalled Enke, Jr.

"We all wanted to come back (he laughed). They already had a reputation."

Upon arriving in New York in preparation for the game and the tournament, Enke Sr., was asked about the team's confidence.

"No, the boys aren't a bit frightened, although naturally a little nervous," Coach Enke told reporters then. "You don't expect fellows with a total of 200 combat missions in China, Africa, Italy, Germany and France to be scared, do you?"

As for the game, Arizona was beaten soundly, 77-53, after trailing 16-1 to start the game. UA didn't hit its first basket until seven minutes into the game. Arizona struggled on a number of fronts. Center Tim Ballantyne fouled out, and UA wasn't used to the 18,000 fans and the game conditions.

"The floor was slippery, and the floor had so many dead spots," said Enke Jr. "We had been playing with a molded ball (in Arizona) and they played with a seamed ball. It didn't bounce as good, so it was tough. It was quite an adjustment.

"We just didn't know what had hit us."

GLASS ACTION

Big-time basketball had escaped Arizona until that season of '46. But it was then that Arizona was good enough to get invited to play in the NIT, the tournament to play in back then.

When they arrived at Madison Square Garden, where the event took place, one of the first things they noticed was the glass backboards. Arizona didn't use them back then.

"Some of our guys would look at them and then shoot clear over the baskets," said Enke Jr. "They'd see them (the crowd) looking right through them, looking at you."

Then there was the case of dealing with the cigar smoke. It was commonplace in MSG back then.

"There were 18,000 people in there, and every man was smoking a cigar," said Marvin Borodkin. "You almost could not see the basket."

PLAYING FOR DAD

Enke was one of Tucson's best high school players in the early 1940s as he was an all-around athlete for Tucson High. But shortly after high school, he was called to the war. Soon after, he left to join his dad on the basketball court.

So how was it playing for his father?

"It was a lot of fun," he said. "It's when we gained prominence. It wasn't strange. I'd flown in the navy so you live dangerously there, too. But it was fun."

He became a three-time all-Border Conference selection.

IT'S COLD, VERY COLD

In the winter of 1946-47, Arizona made a trip to east to face Morehead State in Louisville and then played Miami, Ohio. While in the Midwest, Arizona played games in Detroit against Wayne State and then Michigan State.

What do the guys remember?

It being very cold. And not just because it was snowing.

Arizona won the game 45-43 over a very good Spartan team. UA had a 29-21 lead at halftime, and then staved off a couple of MSU rallies, eventually stalling the ball late to seal the win.

"It was a big field house and they put the floor out in the middle of it and there was no heat," recalled Junior Crum. "Here we are in January and it was absolutely freezing in there. We couldn't take off our sweatsuits sitting on the bench. It's the coldest I ever was."

THE REFS ARE HORRIBLE

During that trip to Michigan, Arizona found out what it meant to face tough referees. After beating Wayne State 59-46 on New Year's Eve in 1946, Arizona faced Michigan State two days later.

"At the end of the game against Wayne State, one of the players said, 'You are two of the more crooked bastards I've ever seen,'" recalled Marvin Borodkin. "Well, guess who the two officials were in the next game against Michigan State? The same two."

Arizona was able to win both games.

RICHMOND READY

For Lincoln Richmond it was an off-and-on career on the Arizona hardwood. But for the 1947–48 season he appeared to be on, despite suffering a knee injury playing football that season. It was his second season after what was a very good sophomore year, having averaged 17.8 points per game. He was perhaps Arizona's first legitimate player who had a chance at All-America honors.

Despite UA's optimism Richmond would play, he played very little because of the knee injury, giving a gritty effort but not the kind they were used to seeing.

Despite the knee problems, Richmond became the first Wildcat player to score more than 1,000 points for a career, finishing with 1,186, a school record that lasted 11 seasons. He was considered one of Enke's all-time best players, becoming the only six-year letter winner in school history.

"He was such a good, tough player," said Fred W. Enke, recalling his longtime friend. "You'd tell him to do something and he'd do it."

Said Honea: "He played with a brace on that knee, but he was very good. He was a very fine shooter and knew the game well. He didn't have many (high) marks his junior or senior year because he was hurt."

Added Crum: "Richmond is probably a guy who could still play nowadays."

Mo Udall—Politician, Star

Morris K. Udall joined UA in 1942, in what he called a "fluke." Yet he was a big contributor to the program, eventually becoming Arizona's first former player to make it to the NBA.

In his book, *Too Funny to be President*, Udall says he was just a third stringer early in his career when in a big game against West Texas—one of Arizona's rivals back then—Enke took out the starting center because he wasn't hustling and inserted Udall. Not fully prepared, Udall didn't last long because he wasn't in great shape. But because the starting center was still pouting for being taken out, Udall was able to take advantage of the situation and returned to play again.

After Mo Udall served his country in WWII and starred for UA on the court, he became Arizona's first player to make it in the NBA.

UDALL, "A LIAR?"

One of the funnier moments during Udall's career came in Albuquerque, New Mexico, when he was having an unbelievable game. And although he said he felt everything he threw up went in, Udall actually went 10 for 23 from the floor and added four free throws. But it was an impressive night, nonetheless. Even the crowd at New Mexico gave him an overwhelming ovation. Yet there were skeptics, specifically one sports writer from Albuquerque who said Udall was a "liar" because "no one shoots like that with a glass eye."

To the sports writer's surprise, Udall "took the slippery orb out of its socket and handed it to him, saying, 'Mister, I haven't been able to see much out of this one, so you try it.'"

Apparently, Udall had pulled that stunt—pulling the eye out—a time or two throughout his Arizona career, often taking it out in practice, or it would just come out.

"Sometimes he'd just lose it," said Fred W. Enke. "It would pop out during practice."

Mostly, Udall, other than being known for being a pretty good basketball player and the class president, was also known as being an affable person.

"He had a dry wit," said Enke. "Everything was funny to him. And if it wasn't, he made it funny. He'd study things and then come up with something."

"He was a real intelligent guy," said Bob Honea. "He liked to joke around. He only had that one eye, but he could shoot it. We'd say that was a good thing because he didn't have to worry about two eyes. He was very talented and athletic."

According to Enke, Udall always ran down the right side of the floor because Udall's blind spot was on the right side. And perhaps the most difficulty Udall had in scoring was in practice.

"We knew which eye was bad, because in practice we'd try to cover his good eye with our hand," Crum said, laughing. "I'm sure the opponents knew he had one eye, but they might not have known which one it was. It was hard to tell, but not if you practiced with him."

A Cut Above

Besides being into athletics, Udall loved dabbling in politics and current events. He was well read and popular. His nickname among his teammates was "Judge."

While in school, he worked cleaning up the dorms and working an odd job—cutting the team's hair.

"He lived at the bottom of the infirmary on campus," said Enke. "He'd sweep up and mop up. That's how he got his room and board at the school. And he'd cut our hair for two bits. When he almost became president we could have said we got haircuts from a two-bit president."

Baylor, a Nemesis

It was an early-season battle between the best the Border Conference had to offer (Arizona) and what the Southwest Conference had (Baylor) in what was the season opener for Arizona. Arizona did what it had to do, beating Baylor 62-54 in front of 3,200 fans at Bear Down Gym. Crum was the star with 14 points.

But that game meant nothing three months later when the teams met again for an NCAA berth in a District 6 playoff. The playoff was Arizona's first taste of the NCAA tournament. As it turned out, Baylor beat Arizona in the best-of-three competition in Dallas and eventually played Kentucky for the national title that spring of 1948.

"It was like playing them on their home court," said Crum, who had 14 points in the first Baylor game.

A season later, Arizona faced Baylor again for the right to advance into the tournament and defeated Baylor 55-47.

"It was such a great experience and honor for me to go into the playoffs and play for the national title," said Honea. "I thought it was great. I went to have fun. Growing up in Marana I hardly kept up with football, basketball or baseball. We had no TV and we didn't get the newspaper. So it was a great experience being from the country."

RECORD SHOWING

The Wildcats must have been peaking at the right time as they headed into the Baylor game. Or so it appeared. The Cats had won nine of 10 games and defeated the Texas El Paso Miners 93-50. The 93 points were a school record at that time. Arizona players felt they were capable of such numbers in that they loved to run. Instead of trying to slow down the Wildcats' fast offense, the Miners decided to run with the Cats. It proved to be a bad decision. Mo Udall had a great game, finishing with 21 points. Link Richmond, still hobbled with an injured knee, added 18.

THE RAZOR IN, THEN OUT

Harold "Razor" Uplinger was a promising player from Los Angeles. He was a good shooter and a savvy player. To begin the 1948 season he just beat out Marana's Honea. But Coach Enke said there would be a battle for their spot all season.

As it turned out, he was right. Through the first month of games, Uplinger played plenty, but by the Christmas break it was Honea who became more of a factor, primarily because he was scoring more points and had an impact on the offensive end.

Eventually, Uplinger decided to leave the team.

"There was a game in there where we got behind and Fred put me in and Uplinger left," Honea said. "He left for Long Island and played when they came through here."

COLD NIGHT IN NY

For many of UA's players it was their first taste of the Big Apple during their eight-game, never-done-before trip to New York City and Madison Square Garden. Arizona fell to St. Francis, 79-70, in front of 18,431 fans in December of 1947. Crum led UA with a game-high 27 points. The points were a single-season record for MSG that year.

"What I remember most is that New York City had one of its worst snowstorms ever the night we played," said Crum. "We were out at one in the morning walking down 42nd street, and there wasn't a car moving."

The snow was perhaps memorable but so was the entire trip. With players mostly all from Arizona, it seemed like a trip of a lifetime.

"It was the first time I had ever been out of Arizona," said Honea, a farm boy from Marana, 20 miles out of Tucson. "It was a great trip. It took three or four days to get there. You'd go to sleep in Texas and wake up in Texas. I was a bit surprised one morning when I found my shoes shined for me. I never even had shoe polish much less had my shoes shined."

Frank A. Enke was ahead of his time in using a run-and-gun style in the 1940s and '50s. He's No. 2 in wins at Arizona with 510.

FUN AND GAMES

On one of Arizona's three trips East, the Arizona players pulled a fast one on Coach Enke. Enke always enjoyed a good game of bridge and the players did, too. On the train they got a game going. Midway through the game, Enke excused himself to go to the restroom, and in the meantime the players stacked the deck so Enke would have 13 spades in his hand. Upon returning to see what he had, he saw the most improbable hand.

"When he came back he was flustered," Enke's son said. "Everybody passed until it got to him. He was trying to keep his composure, and at that time they were playing for one bit. So that's what he bet. ... Eventually he found out he had been had."

THE STREAK

It's a little-known fact, but Arizona is the only school in the country to be part of two huge winning streaks in its history. The first being an 81-game streak began the winter of 1945 (December 14) and ended with a loss to Kansas State almost exactly six years later when Kansas State went into Bear Down and beat UA soundly, 76-57.

"I didn't even realize it," said Bob Honea, who played from 1949-51, of the streak. "We just went out and played. Records didn't mean much to me. I just wanted to play basketball. No one ever put pressure on us."

Said Crum: "I just took it for granted we were going to win."

THE FUTURE OF HOOPS

During a four-game trip east during the 1948 season, Coach Enke and Oklahoma A&M coach Hank Iba got into a discussion about the state of the game. Each had differing views. It all involved the change of the game, going from a two-handed shot to a one-handed shot.

Iba told reporters one-handed shooters weren't as accurate as two-handed shooters and the game's fundamentals were waning because of it. And in part, defenses would collapse on the one-handed shooters, because there was a good chance they'd miss.

"When we meet a team of all one-handed shooters we can afford to set the frontline of our defense a full stride closer to the basket than is advisable against a team carrying as many as two players skilled in the two-handed shot," Iba said. "I predict that in a five-year period we will have defensive basketball, whether we want it or not, to capitalize on the offensive weakness inherent in the long one-handed shot."

Told of Iba's thoughts, Coach Enke replied: "You can't tell the public to be damned. They want a fast, shooting game. The crowds don't come out to see the slow, deliberate defensive club. We believe in using the one-handed shot almost exclusively. It's more accurate and can be gotten away more quickly and it's more spectacular."

WHO IS ENKE?

For one, he's a guy who loved Arizona, having stayed here since the early 1920s. As sports writer Dick Peebles put it, "Enke has found the secret to holding on to a coaching job. He keeps winning. That's just about as good an assurance against getting fired as owning a business and working for yourself."

The guys sure did enjoy playing for him, in part because he understood the players.

"He got along with everyone," said Honea. "He was my fatherly image. If he would have said 'boo,' I would have taken off for the cotton patch. He was just a good guy who watched after us."

But he was a bit quirky. Reports were that he was colorblind—"He sure did dress kind of crazy," Honea said—and he was, by Enke's own words, a bit "superstitious."

He consistently wore his tan jacket and always chewed Doublemint gum.

BEAR DOWN GETS WILD

As Honea remembers it, it was a day the fans "hung from the rafters." And actually the fans did when Arizona faced Arizona State in Bear Down that February 4 night in 1950. Arizona had one of the best teams in the nation back then, was in the middle of its 81-game win streak and was working on its all-time best record at that time. Arizona's 73-51 win set a number of records, including attendance at a basketball game in the state (4,200). Upon further review later, the attendance figures were placed closer to 4,400 people.

SPEED TOPPED

Just a season after saying the game was being improved because of the one-handed shot, Coach Enke felt the game's speed had reached its peak.

Enke told reporters in the early 1950s that the game wouldn't evolve in the next 25 years as much as it did in the previous 25.

"Basketball has reached its peak as far as speed is concerned," Enke told reporters and picked up by the Associated Press. "In the future it will show better ballhandling and more shooting accuracy."

Enke later added: "Teams of today would have little trouble whipping the best of 15 to 25 years ago. Today's squads are better trained and have more basketball knowledge because of the sport's growth."

IN OR OUT?

Arizona was rolling along in 1950, playing to a 24-2 record in the season's final two weekends when it ventured off to the Texas panhandle and lost two of three. After the defeats it was thought Arizona would miss on a chance to return to the postseason. Its consecutive streak of five Border Conference titles was in jeopardy. What it had to do was beat Hardin-Simmons at home to win the title. If they got a tournament bid, so be it.

Arizona proceeded to beat Hardin-Simmons 63-41 to finish the regular season 26-4 and 14-2 in the conference. That same week, Arizona was invited to participate in the NIT for the third time in five years. It was easily declared Arizona's all-time best season to date and its clear rise to a national power.

The night Arizona won the title in beating Hardin-Simmons, none other than Cleveland Indians star pitcher Bob Feller was in attendance. Back then, the Indians made Tucson their spring training home. When asked about the game and an officiating crew that seemed to call fouls on a whim, Feller said, "I don't know about the officiating, but I know that Arizona beat the hell out of Hardin-Simmons."

Indeed.

BE NICE—PLEASE

In the Hardin-Simmons game, then-school athletic director J.F. McKale urged fans in attendance to be polite to the visiting team. He did so after news reports out of Abilene, Texas, said Enke and Arizona were the ones who had Hardin-Simmon's player Julius Stagner declared ineligible earlier in the season. In an earlier trip to Abilene, Coach Enke was hit in the face with a wet towel. Clearly, there was no love lost between the two schools.

"No question that he watched the players," said Honea, of Coach Enke. "If he thought he was getting hoodwinked by any of the players—or a visiting team—he stood right up for us."

YOU'RE FUNNY

When Arizona made its trek to New York City to play in the NIT in 1950, it was a first for many UA players to be in New York. It was a first for Honea.

After all, here was the "Mayor of Marana" in Metropolis for the first time, walking among the skyscrapers.

"That was an experience," said Honea. "We left Tucson right after breakfast and got to Chicago and had lunch and I said, 'That's pretty good.' We left and got somewhere else and had a snack, and I said, 'That's pretty good.' Then we got to New York to have dinner and someone said, 'That's pretty good.'"

Sure was. When Honea stepped off the plane teammate Leo Johnson said, "Small-town boy comes to the big city."

Honea quickly replied: "Heck, Leo, that's what they say about you when you go into Safford (a small town in Arizona)."

Honea recalled later that Johnson "liked to joke friendly. He's a good guy; a good rebounder. He held that team together."

Honea helped by shooting well.

"One of the guys said, 'Honea has been throwing cotton balls into a bucket for years, so he has no problem with a basketball.'"

NIT NOT TO BE

Upon arriving in New York, not many people thought Arizona would beat LaSalle. For one thing, not much was known about the Cats, despite their 26-4 record.

But one man did. It was famed college coach Pete Newell, then the coach of NIT defending-champ San Francisco.

"Arizona has an excellent chance of beating LaSalle," Newell told the Associated Press. "It should be a very good game. Both clubs are very fast. LaSalle will be the best team Arizona has met this season. If Fred Enke can devise a way to stop Larry Foust (LaSalle's six-foot-nine center) the Wildcats have half the battle won. But if Arizona is hitting as it showed it could in beating St. Mary's, the Wildcats can take the game."

Easier said than done. Arizona fell 72-66. Foust finished with 14 points. Arizona had two leads in the second half, before foul trouble and a late rally was cut short. Arizona struggled on the MSG floor, reporting a number of dead spots on the court and not being used to playing there.

"All I remember was that plank floor we played on, and it was cold," said Honea, who had 16 points in the game. "It was tough. But it was exciting."

PLAYING OPOSSUM

To begin the 1950-51 season, Coach Enke figured his team would finish no better than seventh in the Border Conference race. What? Arizona had just won its sixth straight conference and appeared ready to get No. 7. But Enke tempered everyone's excitement with his prediction of a seventh. His figuring was the team lost Leo Blevins, a talented scorer, and Paul Penner, a solid 6-7 center, from the previous year, so there would be struggles.

Hardly. UA went 15-1 for its best record in conference play. UA eventually finished 24-6 and arguably had one of, if not the best teams in school history that season.

POINT SHAVING

Arizona headed east for one its most ambitious trips in school history. It left Tucson undefeated at 6-0. First stop was at Canisius, where UA lost 55-52 after a late rally fell short. But the headline game was the next one against tough City College of New York.

What a Madison Square Garden crowd of 18,000 fans saw was unbelievable. Arizona stayed close, eventually pulling out a remarkable 41-38 win in what Coach Enke called his "greatest victory of my career."

Midway through the second half, the game was tied at 35. But then Arizona slowly pulled away for the win.

Coach Enke, whose team relied more on speed than cunning, decided to slow the game down against the defending national champions. And it seemed to have worked.

Seemed?

Well, at least three CCNY players were part of a "fix" on the game. CCNY threw other games as well. What it did was give a black eye to college basketball and sports in general.

"It didn't really deflate us," said Honea, of the news CCNY may have fixed the game. "We were excited that we had won. We couldn't tell that they tried to do what they did. It was a tough game."

Apparently, one of the criteria for CCNY players to pull off the fix was they needed to keep the game within three points either way. And if they lost, it was even better.

NEVER GOING BACK

After knocking off CCNY, UA was on a clear high. Two days later it would come crashing down as Duquesne edged the Cats 65-63. But not without some controversy.

Four Arizona players fouled out in the final 10 minutes. Trying to preserve a lead, UA players started playing "stall ball" on Duquesne, but even then the hometown officials were calling fouls that weren't fouls, Enke claimed.

The officiating was so bad, Honea reportedly went up to an official and told him he had worked a horrible game. And with it, he'd never take his team back to play there again. And he didn't.

"At that Duquesne game some guy said to me, 'You'll never win it. The refs won't let you win,'" recalled Honea. "And we lost. It was pathetic."

BIG GAME

One of the bigger games of the 1950s came when Long Island University came to Tucson. And as was the sign of the times, there was controversy. First, LIU officials said they were not going to send a team to Tucson after then-Arizona congressman Harold A. Patten was heard heckling the LIU team in a December game at the Garden. Arizona played CCNY in a double header there. LIU played Western Kentucky.

Patten had reportedly said, "They look like a bunch of Harlem Globetrotters."

Patten also admitted getting on LIU coach Claire Bee at that game, with Bee saying if he was younger he'd have gone after the congressman.

Feeling LIU players might be in danger in Arizona, the Blackbirds called to say they were not going to make the trip. LIU feared for the safety of its black players if that was the attitude of people in Arizona. But after speaking to UA officials, LIU, with three black players, made the trip.

"I hope that every Towncat here will make it his special business to see that LIU … goes home from Tucson saying that it has never enjoyed fairer treatment," wrote Dr. Floyd Thomas, then chairman of UA's committee for intercollegiate athletics.

Then came the game where it was expected to draw the biggest crowd for a basketball game in the state's history. More than 5,000 fans were expected. Back then the price of the must-have ticket was $1.50. It was to put the Wildcats on the basketball map.

It also marked the return of former UA player Uplinger, who left UA after one semester in 1948. He had since transferred to LIU.

"On the surface we were glad to see each other," said Honea, who had usurped Uplinger's position back then. "But the rivalry was deep. The fans knew of it. He had more basketball savvy than I did, but I could shoot the ball."

In the end, Arizona came back from an 18-point, first-half deficit. It was Jerome Dillon's free throw with 15 seconds left that gave UA a 62-61 win over the fourth-ranked Blackbirds in front of 4,650 fans (then a record). Uplinger finished with nine points; Honea with 14. The next week UA was ranked 13th, the highest in school history.

But again it wasn't without controversy. LIU's Bee claimed the referees took the game away from his team, "just as everyone on the west coast said they would. You'll never get any good teams to play here for that reason. If I had the greatest ball club in the world, I wouldn't be able to beat Arizona here."

And that was coming from a coach who hadn't lost a home game at LIU in 13 seasons, a span of 139 games. Bee knew all about home-court advantages. Realizing that, Bee declared he'd start taking his team more and more on the road, even perhaps playing UA in Tucson again some day.

It never happened.

WOODEN VS. ENKE

The setting? Well, Arizona faced UCLA at the Cow Palace in San Francisco for a four-team tournament. But back then it was Enke Sr., who was more known than the now-famous John Wooden. After all, Arizona was perhaps the premier team in the West having won a number of Border Conference titles in a row, and proving itself on its trip east. It was Wooden's fourth year as the head coach at UCLA.

Arizona lost that game 69-63.

"We should have beaten them," said Honea. "We were the best team in the West at that time. It was a great day, we just didn't have a good game."

Chapter 3

1950s-1970s

A NIGHT OUT

It was the start of the New Year in 1953 and UA was struggling, having lost four of six games to begin the 1952-53 season.

It would only get worse when Arizona traveled east to participate in the Memphis Invitational in Memphis, Tennessee.

"We had played Ole Miss in a hell of a game," said former UA player George Rountree, speaking of a 75-70 loss in the first round. "We were down 22 and came back in the second half. Late in the game, we were on a three-on-two break with 40 seconds left and one point down. Rudy Castro was bringing the ball down with Allan Stanton coming down the right side and me on the left, and Castro decided to get a bounce pass to Stanton. He (Stanton) had bad knees from playing football, so he made a cut to the goal for a layup but his knee went out from under him, and the ball went out of bounds. We lost the game."

Coach Enke was livid. But not as mad as he was the next night when UA played host to Memphis State.

"We lost by 20 or something (75-56), and Fred was so angry," Rountree said. "I was not happy having lost the game. I was in the locker room musing over what I did wrong and how I could have helped the team. Fred came in and said, 'The bus is leaving, and I don't care how you get back to the hotel.' Some people got on the bus, but some of us had to walk back to the hotel."

HEY, ISN'T THAT ...

Arizona made a trip east for a four-game swing through the northeast, playing four games in a week. It played at Bradley, Beloit, Canisius and Niagra during the New Year's holiday.

After beating Canisius for its only win of the four games, the players decided they'd celebrate somehow.

"We were in Buffalo and I had a good game," Rountree said. "Several of us decided to go to a bar. We had a curfew of about 12:30, so we were all there for that, but at one in the morning we all sneaked out. When we got there and sat down, I heard this snicker behind me. It was Fred."

Apparently, silence was golden.

"(Later in the night) we got up and walked up and nodded at him, and he nodded back and never said anything about it."

But according to Bill Smitheran, the next day Enke got his team up early so they could go to Niagra Falls.

"We weren't feeling too well because some were blitzed from the night before," Smitheran said. "It was snowy and cold. But Fred got us up to go. Fred never held anything against you, but he had a clever way of getting at you."

IT WASN'T ME

Rountree clearly was a practical joker, a smart aleck of sorts.

One day in Abilene, Texas, Rountree, while in his hotel room and up a few stories, saw Enke walking on the sidewalk. Rountree's roommate Jim Brower had some firecrackers with him—cherry bombs—so Rountree set one off and sent it flying. It landed about 10 feet from Enke.

"You would have thought the damn building went down," Rountree said. "He rushed up and pounded on the door. He was saying, 'All right, Rountree what are you doing?' He was uptight. I yelled at him, 'Coach, I'm asleep.'" But Enke wanted in and he wanted answers.

"I had all my clothes on and Brower was taking a nap," Rountree added. "I went into the bathroom, turned on the shower and took off my clothes. I had Brower get the door. I came out of the shower and patted myself dry."

Enke was furious.

"Rountree," Enke said, "I know that was you. Nobody on the team would do that but you. You ought not to play tonight."

Rountree, a quick wit, said, "Actually it was probably God sending you a message that we might win tonight." Enke smiled and turned around and left.

YOU PULLED A SHOE

On long trips via the bus, the team would often play poker to pass the time. One player, Tom Shoemaker, usually was asked to participate—for a reason.

"Tom Shoemaker had more money than anyone on the team," Rountree recalled. "His father was a cotton farmer in the Casa Grande area."

On one trip to West Texas, Bill Kemmeries, James Dunlap, Jackson Eddy and Shoemaker got a game going. It was the usual seven-card stud.

Through five cards Kemmeries was showing three queens and Shoemaker was showing two jacks.

"But Shoe raises Kemmeries on the sixth card. And by this time the pot was $12 to $15, which was big money back then," Rountree said. "Then Shoe gets another jack so he raises again."

Obviously Kemmeries won, "but Shoemaker looked dejected, like he didn't know that three jacks didn't beat three queens."

From then on when players made crazy plays on cards they called it "a shoe."

"It was a non-winning bet," Rountree said. "Shoe's in."

Happy New Year

Arizona was going through one of its all-time worst losing streaks under Enke midway through the 1956 season having lost eight consecutive games. During that time, UA took a trip east, playing Louisville, Ohio University, Bowling Green and Murray State. All were losses.

Two days after losing to Bowling Green in its final game of the Kentucky Invitational on New Year's Eve, some UA players decided to go out and have some fun. They figured they were due. Among the leaders was Bob Mueller.

"We went looking for some refreshments ... beer," Mueller said. "But we were in a dry county in Kentucky."

So off they went to Tennessee, not returning back to the hotel until about 3:30 a.m.

Enke was waiting for them. And of course, he was mad.

"We honked at him, waved and then went to have breakfast," Mueller said, laughing.

It didn't go without consequences.

"He ripped us a new one, saying this was why we were not winning any games. We needed to take things seriously. He made us run two extra laps in practice the next day."

So would he do it all over again?

"Absolutely," he said.

MIKEY LIKES IT

Long before there was Mikey from those Life cereal commercials there was Bill Reeves, a six-foot-four forward.

On a trip to Salt Lake City, one morning at breakfast Reeves ate like a champ.

"Breakfast was the only meal where you could eat what you wanted because the other meals were always planned out," Rountree said. "Reeves had pancakes, eggs, bacon, sausage, toast and juice. There were all kinds of plates around Reeves at the end of the meal. It looked so bizarre that some of the guys decided to put their used plates in front of his so it looked like he had eaten enough for a platoon."

Guess who happens along? Enke.

"Fred looks at the table then looks at Reeves, and then says, 'Damn boy, eat like Notre Dame and play like Po-dunk.'"

HADIE REDD, A PIONEER

It wasn't easy for Hadie Redd, Arizona's first African American men's basketball player. In the 1950s, he was criticized and ridiculed on most every road trip. Trips to Texas were seemingly unbearable. Opposing fans got on him constantly.

"One game we played at Texas Tech and they couldn't seat very many and they were close to the floor," recalled Rountree. "When we ran out on the floor they'd say, 'Go back to Tucson, you black bastard. We don't want you here.'"

Of course, other words—not so kind—were being yelled, as well.

Hadie Redd made history at UA when he became the first African-American basketball player at the school.

There were games when Redd was so shaken he played poorly. But his teammates admired him.

On a trip to Texas, one fast-food place didn't want to serve Redd, so they all left. Bill Smitheran and Bill Reeves, teammates and friends, said it happened on more than one occasion.

"We never really talked about that stuff," said Rountree. "I thought Fred Enke treated him very nice. But I'm not sure he knew how to deal with it. It was very difficult for Hadie to deal with."

McCray Troubles

After was Hadie Redd came Ernie McCray, one of UA's all-time great basketball players of any era. He too suffered problems because he was an African American growing up in the 1950s.

"I never had a problem with playing with the guys at all," said McCray. "There was no racial tension at all."

That's not to say he didn't experience it in Tucson, a town that still had its problems with race relations.

"The cops stopped me a few times," said McCray, a Tucson native. "That was just a time when cops were basically hassling black people. But the one thing I appreciated in Tucson—although they had some (racist) stuff, you could curse a cop. It wasn't like the south and they'd hang you from a tree. I'd call them things. I knew the law and they sensed that."

McCray recalled one instance when, while running home after practice, he was stopped by cops and asked what he was running from.

"I remember coming from the Stone Avenue underpass and a group of people in a car yelled out, 'Nigger' to me. I just yelled back at them, cursing at them."

Well, a policeman, tending to a hurt dog, heard the commotion and got on McCray for cursing in public.

"He was like, 'If it weren't for the dog I'd take you in,'" McCray said.

"I was like, 'Yeah, right.'"

HOTEL TROUBLES

While Redd had to stay with black families while on the road, McCray didn't.

About four years had passed, and McCray didn't have it as bad as Redd had it. But there were still underlying problems. Some even blatant.

On a trip to Abilene, Texas, McCray was given a room that wasn't up to standards.

"They gave me a room that when you turned the water on it was a gold color from all the rust in the pipes," McCray said.

On another occasion while playing in west Texas, McCray, and some other players, were invited to attend a party after a game. So the guys showed up.

"It was one of the first times I had ever been invited to go to a party," McCray said.

"I thought, 'Wow.' While there I approached a white girl to dance and all of a sudden it seemed like I was EF Hutton— it was so quiet. I was like, 'Oh shit, what did I just do?'"

LARSON IN

By 1958, Enke had seen better days. Or least he had seen more consistent winning ways. So on February 21, 1958, he let it slip out that he'd likely retire when he reached 65. Then again, that was the age of retirement for UA department heads.

Back then, he hinted that it likely was a near lock that one of his former UA players would succeed him. But who would it be?

Maybe Leo Johnson. Maybe Billy Mann or Bill Kemmeries. Or was it going to be Bruce Larson?

As it turned out three years later, it was Larson, who played in 1949 and 1950, before embarking on a career as a successful junior college coach (Eastern Arizona) and coach at Weber JC in Ogden, Utah.

After one of Arizona's worst seasons—4-22—Larson was named Enke's assistant, a big move back then.

"This is by far the biggest step forward for basketball in the 34 years I've been here," Enke said, at the time.

That said, UA's athletic administrators gave the basketball program $2,000 for recruiting, something they had never done before.

WHAT COACH?

Long before Cedric Dempsey was the school's athletic director, he was a former assistant coach in the '60s. At that time he was in charge of the freshman team. Against Cochise Junior College he became so frustrated at halftime that he struggled to come up with a word to use to get the guys fired up.

"I said, 'You guys are so lethargic,'" Dempsey said, as part of his speech to his players.

As the team returned to the floor, Gordon Lindstrom held up his hand and said, "Before we go back on the floor could you tell us what lethargic means?"

McCray Hits Bottle, Record

It was the start of the decade but the end of the 1959-60 season when McCray was ending his solid career. Then came the night of February 6, 1960.

Arizona faced Los Angeles State in Tucson and Bear Down Gym and McCray finished with a school-record 46 points in a 104-84 victory. The record still stands.

The 104 points also established a new school record.

As McCray broke the old school record of 38 points (set by Teddy Lazovich in 1954) the crowd of 2,055 cheered his every move and basket. At one point when he got his 40th point to break the record, the crowd cheered so much play was interrupted.

Little did anyone know that McCray had a secret. Before the game—at his home—he had drank alcohol before the game to ease his mind.

"What happened was that it was one of the most incredibly stupid things a person could do," McCray said. "I had done some wild things, but that wasn't a pattern of mine (to drink before a game). But I was feeling pressure with those records, and my wife and I weren't getting along at the time. And then there were exams."

Buddies came along with wine. And everyone drank.

"I was so ashamed," he said. "When I was going to the game I was thinking to myself, 'You have to straighten up. Be ready.' I think I entered a new level of focus. I just couldn't let anyone know what was going on."

More than 40 years later, McCray still holds the record, with it having a chance to fall just a couple of times. Most recently by Damon Stoudamire, who had a career-high 45 points in a win against Stanford in 1995.

"It doesn't matter if it's broken; I'm a UA fan and I root for the guys," McCray said. "If someone breaks it, that would be fun. I've had my fun with it for almost 50 years."

Ernie McCray could do it all. He still holds the scoring record for points in a game with 46.

ODD MOVE

In early January of 1960, Arizona was going through its sixth consecutive nonwinning season. Fans were discouraged. Students were too. Finally, the sports editor of the campus newspaper, Jesus Barker, editorialized that Enke should resign.

Barker wrote, "Since the end of the 1950-51 season, our total record stands at 64 wins against 115 losses, and there is no relief in sight." Barker wrote of team discord, and that perhaps Enke's time had come and gone.

But Enke remained steadfast he wasn't going to resign or retire. He was to be 63, and mandatory retirement age was 65.

Ironically, however, despite continued criticism, Enke did something unusual when the season ended. He hired Barker to join his staff. The hire no less happened on April Fools Day. He was hired as publicity director for the team. Of course, Barker's tune changed.

"Mr. Enke is a fine coach and gentleman. During his 35 years as basketball coach he has turned out some highly regarded teams," Barker said, back then. "Next season, as far as I can see, should be no exception."

LOOK OUT BELOW

Playing at New Mexico was always fun—and interesting—for Warren Rustand, arguably one of Arizona's best players in the 1960s. Never mind he went 2-4 in his time against the Lobos. The famed "Pit" was always an adventure.

"In one game someone threw an aerosol spray can out from the stands," Rustand said. "It hit the official, and he went down like he had been shot."

But having a spray can thrown down was just one of the many objects teams had to endure in Albuquerque.

Guard Warren Rustand was one of the smartest—and best— guards in Wildcat history.

"They'd throw hot pennies and they seemed to have a high intelligence about the players," he added.

"Like who we were dating and everything."

NO BOUNCE

By the mid-1960s, Bear Down Gym was 40 years old.

And it had been one of the oldest and more worn facilities in the West—if not the nation. But there were always constants in the gym—like dead spots on the floor. Arizona players took advantage of the homecourt advantage.

"It was built on springs so you could jump well," Rustand said. "But there were also a series of dead spots. We knew where they were from practicing in there. We'd try to guide our man in that direction.

"And the basketball would not come up, so that would create turnovers and we'd take advantage of that. Some things would happen to us if we weren't paying attention."

AIRSICKNESS BAG PLEASE

As former UA assistant coach Cedric Dempsey recalled it was a "pretty intense trip."

Heading to Denver via Laramie, Wyoming, there was blowing snow and ice. All the conditions that make flying scary in any era.

"We were heading to Denver," Rustand recalled. "Albert Johnson hadn't flown a great deal. We were about halfway to Denver when there was a crack in the emergency door, or it had opened a bit."

People panicked.

"Albert Johnson (who is African American) was white for about an hour," Rustand said. "Everyone else was going to the bathroom and throwing up. Everyone thought the plane was going down. Johnson was gripping the armrests so hard he dislodged them from their seat he was so scared."

Johnson said Rustand had quite an imagination. Johnson said everyone was scared, including Rustand, who at one point locked himself in the restroom.

"It was quite an experience, particularly when the pilot said he needed to depressurize and fly low over the Grand Canyon," Johnson said. "We were bouncing over the air like a dove in the wind. There weren't enough airsickness bags in the plane to take care of everybody."

As for turning white, Johnson said it was more like Rustand "turning green."

CLOSE BUT ...

Being part of the Western Athletic Conference at the time, Arizona had a chance to face Texas Western and the "Bear," Don Haskins, twice a year. In 1965-66, UA had a chance to make a bit of history, although it wouldn't know it at the time. In El Paso, Arizona played the Miners tough, eventually going into overtime before losing 81-72.

"And we did it on their homecourt," Michael Aboud said. Later that season, Texas Western beat Kentucky for the NCAA title.

But Aboud remembers the game for another reason. During the game, he was hit hard in the head and knocked out.

"Out of the corner of my eye I saw this hand coming toward me. He had cold-cocked me across the mouth," Aboud said. "He busted my lip. It caught me by surprise, and I was stunned. I took some time before the cobwebs were out."

What Abound found out later was that his teammate, Harvey Fox, had been elbowing that Miner player all night.

"I guess the guy thought it was me. I guess we both look alike," Abound said.

IT'S COLD

Wyoming is notorious for being one of the coldest states in the country. At least Arizona players found that out in early January of 1965. The temperature was well below zero, and the wind chill was 56 below, according to Albert Johnson.

"We went to practice in the fieldhouse and there were no heaters or furnaces," he said. "We all practiced in long johns and sweatsuits."

After the practice, Johnson said coach Bruce Larson wanted the team to go for a walk. The guys looked at Larson "like he was crazy."

"We walked out those turn-style doors of the hotel and came right back through them. We then went straight to our rooms," Johnson said. "It was just too cold to walk."

BUOYED AT BYU

During a trip to Brigham Young University, Monte Clausen and a couple of teammates decided to go out in Provo. Clausen met some girls who attended BYU. They eventually stayed out late.

"Nothing happened, but we did get back after the curfew," said Clausen, who was the son of Dick Clausen, the

Former player Bruce Larson replaced Fred A. Enke as coach but couldn't find long-term success.

school's athletic director. "No one really knew. We weren't too sure if Larson knew it."

Larson knew.

"We met for breakfast and Larson came over and said, 'Monte, did you have fun last night?' I said, 'Yes.' And then he proceeded to say that he didn't want to start me, but that he would anyway. But he added that if at any point I looked tired, he was going to take me out and I would stay out."

As it turned out, Clausen said, "I had one of my best games of the year. I was so afraid not to. Also, my being the AD's son may have put some pressure on Bruce."

"THE FOX" ARRIVES

UA athletic director Dave Strack took a gamble in 1971 on hiring (1) an assistant coach to replace Bruce Larson as head coach; and (2) an African American, college basketball's first. The move proved to be genius. Fred "the Fox" Snowden returned Arizona basketball to prominence. Snowden almost didn't take the job, deciding nearly at the last minute that he enjoyed his job under then-coach Johnny Orr at Michigan. Finally, Snowden decided otherwise.

He'd take the chance. After a press conference announcing his hiring, Snowden cried, realizing his hiring was a major step for not only him but for African American coaches.

"He was very underappreciated," said Bob Elliott, one of Snowden's and the school's stars. "He's the one that lit the fire here. We played to sold out crowds at McKale Center in the mid-'70s."

Elliott still believes had it not been for Snowden's success, Arizona coach Lute Olson would not have come to UA in the early 1980s.

"I totally believe that," Elliott said. "Lute had a choice of any program he wanted. And he came to Arizona. He saw what could be done. And back in the day, the crowds were so loud your eardrums would hurt. It was deafening."

In Snowden's first five years at McKale Center, he was 62-3, at one point winning 38 consecutive games.

It didn't come without problems. Players reported—after Snowden's death in 1994—Snowden constantly received death threats. And Strack received calls saying he'd made a horrible hire, mostly because Snowden was African-American.

"Fred revolutionized basketball here. He fathered the tradition that has become McKale," said John Schaefer, who was then the president of UA.

Playing with Pain

Arizona was coming off one of its all-time best seasons in 1976. It had tons of talent in Jim Rappis, Herman Harris, Al Fleming and Bob Elliott. It lost to UCLA in the West Regional semifinals in Los Angeles.

There were high hopes for UA the following year in part because Elliott and Harris were back, among others.

But little did anyone know Elliott played injured the entire season, eventually finding it was a torn cartilage.

"Two weeks before the season I twisted my left knee in practice, and I knew I needed surgery," Elliott said. "And back then it wasn't like they were running around handing out MRIs."

Elliott decided to play injured. After all, Arizona needed him—badly. And if he went under the knife he felt it would have hurt his NBA career.

Bob Elliott finds the basket for two of his then-record 2,155 career points.

"We just elected to keep it quiet," Elliott said. "I literally played my senior year left handed because I couldn't jump off my left leg."

Luckily, Elliott was ambidextrous and was able to pull it off.

"They'd let me go left," he said, demonstrating a left look, "and I'd say, 'Thank you.'"

As it turned out he was a decoy most of his senior year despite scoring 430 points, 165 fewer points than the previous season.

Elliott sat out one game because of overuse.

"Freddie used the excuse that I was mentally drained that day," Elliott said. "Everyone knew I wasn't taking basket-weaving classes."

After a first-round loss in the NCAAs to Southern Illinois—he had surgery. And still no one knew.

"I went to St. Mary's Hospital under a different name," he said. "The only ones that knew were the surgeons and the anesthesiologist."

A TALL ORDER

Elliott was listed at six foot 10. He was Arizona's all-everything, who eventually was the school's all-time leading scorer until Sean Elliott (no relation) came around 10 years later.

"Freddie always lied about everybody's height," Elliott said. "I've never been 6-10. I don't know if I was 6-10 with my Afro. My high school coach lied about my height. I told him once that I'm not even 6-9."

Elliott said Freddie told him, "You'll grow into it."

"Funny thing was that Freddie had an Afro rule on how big your Afro could be, but it didn't apply to me," said Elliott.

"The longer the Afro, the less people really knew where the head ended or my hair started."

SCARY SITUATION

With just under a minute left in a game between Arizona and host Utah, a bomb scare was called in on February 18, 1977. Arizona was down 76-61 and had no chance to win. Then came the game announcer, "Ladies and gentlemen, at the conclusion of today's game, will people file out as quickly as possible. A bomb threat has been called in." No sooner had the announcement been made, and Elliott looked to Snowden and said, "It's time to go."

"We were getting beat by double digits, and I'm supposed to hang around for another two minutes?" Elliott asked. "To see a bomb go off? I told Freddie that he could stay, but that I was out of there. The other guys followed me. It just didn't make any sense to stay. They agreed."

The game was eventually called after the Wildcats had put their street clothes over their jerseys.

Was a bomb found? "Don't know and don't care," Elliott said. "We were back at the hotel safe."

No bomb was found.

HERMAN HURT

Herman Harris, one of the most athletic players ever at UA, joined the team in 1974. While messing around with Elliott, he threw a football that traveled 70 yards.

"Up until the time he hurt his ankle, he did some things that were unheard of," said Elliott. "I hadn't seen anyone in Arizona basketball do what he did. He was so athletic."

As Elliott described it, Harris was a rock at six foot five, 220 pounds.

"He'd take off from the free-throw line and dunk. He had hands like Dr. J and could dunk. He shot three-pointers (the distance), and people would swear he was out of bounds."

Despite an ankle injury during the 1974-75 season that sidelined Harris, Arizona didn't miss a beat, going 11-1 through the early part of January.

The injury was a complete dislocation, so bad you could see the stub of his foot.

"It didn't tear any of the ligaments or tendons, it just stretched them all," Harris said.

"Typical of Herm," Elliott said, "he said a line out of a movie—'Don't call me an ambulance, call me a cab.'"

The injury didn't stop Harris, but it did slow him.

"He didn't go with that reckless abandon he used to," Elliott said. "Part of the reason why he was so powerful of a player and yet so graceful was because he was fearless. He'd attempt to do things none of us would dream of."

GIVE ME THE BALL

No matter the era, Arizona players still wanted to be the man when it came to points and rebounds.

That was the case in 1977, when Arizona made its second consecutive trip to the NCAA tournament.

Arizona faced Southern Illinois in Omaha, Nebraska.

"We were down at halftime, and the players were going at one another," recalled Joe Nehls, then a freshman. "It was Herman (Harris), Gilbert (Myles) and Bob (Elliott). It was like

Shaquile O'Neal and Kobe Bryant of today. They wanted the ball, and here I was this freshman at my first NCAA tournament. But Bob was the one who was right, because he was virtually unstoppable."

What surprised Nehls was the bickering.

"It was all news to me," he said. "Here I was just a freshman making my first road trip. But once Freddy (Snowden) got in the locker room, everything came to a halt. It got real quiet. No one said anything after that."

Arizona eventually lost the game, 81-77.

From WAC to PAC

Arizona went big time in 1978. The Wildcats, along with Arizona State, made the jump from the Western Athletic Conference to the Pacific 10 Conference. Everyone involved was thrilled about the challenge.

The Cats met the challenge immediately.

In facing the Bruins, then the No. 2 team in the nation, Arizona stunned UCLA when John Smith hit one of two free throws and David Greenwood missed his jumper from the corner for a 70-69 win.

"That was just one of those games where we had a feeling we'd win," said Nehls, the team's starting guard. "They were great. But we just had a feeling."

Four days later UA beat a tough USC team, 74-72. What the victories did was reinforce UA's belief it belonged in the conference.

"That was a good transition," Nehls said. "It helped a lot."

UA finished 16-11 and 10-8 in conference.

"Those were some great days for us," said Robbie Dosty.

And a time when UA moved into the big time.

And playing in UCLA's Pauley Pavilion was always special. After all, it's the house that John Wooden built.

"All those banners up there—it's just amazing and intimidating," said Nehls.

Then there was the day they met Wooden. He walked through practice one day.

"I'm sure it was a ploy on their part, but Wooden walked across, and our practice just stopped," Dosty said. "Everyone was just in awe of him. I knew I wasn't going to practice any more until I got a chance to meet him."

Nehls felt the same way.

"Coach Snowden knew Coach Wooden, so he was at the practice watching us," Nehls said. "I was probably awestruck more than anyone, because I had been a big fan of UCLA basketball. After practice I ran to the bookstore and got a bunch of UCLA memorabilia. Jerry Holmes (UA's assistant back then) said, 'How are you going to play against UCLA when you get all the UCLA memorabilia?'"

Chapter 4

EARLY 1980s

ON A MISSION

Just days after Olson was named the head coach, one of the first recruits the Wildcats brought in was junior college transfer Pete Williams. Williams was being recruited by Colorado, Texas Christian and Nevada Las Vegas.

"I was in the car with Coach (Scott) Thompson, and then all of a sudden there was this dust storm that kicked up," Williams recalled. "I turned to him and said, 'It looks like you're on a mission to rebuild Arizona basketball.' And he said, 'That's exactly what we're going to do.'

"And he's done just that. He's built a monster here—it's unreal what Coach Olson has done. I watched him there and I know what he did. But never in my wildest dreams did I think it would take off the way it did."

Williams the Cornerstone

Olson credits Williams as being THE guy who started UA's success. Sure, there have been many to follow with Steve Kerr, Sean Elliott, Damon Stoudamire, et al.

Fred "The Fox" Snowden, college basketball's first African-American coach at the Division I level, proved Arizona could be a basketball hotbed.

But without Williams there would not have been an Elliott, and so on.

"The way that the program was when we arrived, I don't think Sean was thinking about Arizona," Olson said. "Pete was the best player while he was here for two years. He was also a great recruiter."

Williams is flattered with being credited for helping turn everything around.

"That makes me feel good to hear that," he said. "But I don't want to shortchange anyone. He got me so late (in the recruiting process), maybe that's why it's such a big deal to Coach."

It may have been guard Michael Tate who lured Williams to Tucson. The two, both Californians, were part of UA's first recruiting class. Tate had already signed with UA, convincing Williams UA was the place to be.

"Eddie (Smith), Mike and Reggie (Miller) all came together on a recruiting trip," said Williams. "And Mike said it was great. He was filling up my head with things. I couldn't wait to get down there. I was already a Pac-10 fan to begin with."

A year later, however, Tait left the program, after being beaten out by Brock Brunkhorst for a starting guard spot.

"People never really found out how good of a player Michael Tate was," said Williams. "Had he stayed here, I believe he would have had a long-lasting NBA career."

Earlier in the season, Arizona had lost another player—the talented Richard Hollis, who quit the team. Olson said, Hollis "was not ready for a disciplined program."

Part of Hollis's problem was he couldn't make time on a mandatory run that all players had to do.

"We all had to do it, he just couldn't," Williams said.

Hollis eventually transferred to Houston.

"People in Tucson really missed on something special," Williams said.

Said former assistant coach Thompson: "He had a hard time with discipline. I was the one out there running him. Years later I became the head coach at Rice and he was at Houston, so we faced him all the time. He'd come out and have the best games against us."

First Practice ... Hell

It took nearly four hours for Olson to make his point about where Arizona needed to go—and how far.

"I remember we were out there forever," said Steve Kerr, speaking of the first practice, one that lasted three hours, 45 minutes. "He kept telling us how bad we were. And we were bad. But he laid down the law early. He was tough on us. We worked hard, because we knew we had to get things going. And he had to instill discipline."

That was perhaps the least of UA's problems.

"We had a lot of work to do," Olson said. "I did feel the potential was here, that the climate, the university and the facilities were plus factors. I thought it could get done here. But the program was further down than I thought."

Practices, at times, were so difficult to get through, even free throws presented a problem. Back then, Olson had them make 10 free throws before they were allowed to get a drink of water.

"Usually it takes just a few minutes and you're ready to go," recalled Thompson. "We sat there for 20 to 30 minutes waiting for them to make free throws. We (coaches) just shook our heads at that."

Said Williams: "We were bad, but look what they were coming off of (4-24 season). It was a horrible experience for everybody. You had to learn how to win.

"I remember watching (UA) the season before while in junior college and remembering saying, 'These guys are horrible.' It was a learning process, and it took some time. Look where we were when the season ended."

COME SEE US

Former UA coach Ben Lindsey not only left the program in a shambles but also the fan base was all but left emotionally bankrupt after the 4-24 season in '84. So Olson and his coaches took it upon themselves to go out and recruit fans. It wasn't surprising to see them at city functions and fraternity houses on campus.

"One time we wanted to drum up some enthusiasm because the students weren't coming to the games," said Thompson. "We went around to some fraternity houses and I'll never forget Lute speaking to one group. Imagine having him doing that now. There was a group of about 15 guys and Lute talks about his team and the guys—Kerr, Williams and talked about their enthusiasm."

After Olson was done, he asked the students if they had any questions.

"After a long pause, one guy raised his hand and said, 'Can we bring coolers to the game?' The guy didn't even care about the game," Thompson said.

TRAVEL FOR PUBLICITY

During that first year, in order to get some interest going, UA played in far-away places like Nogales, Coolidge, and Casa Grande. Anything and everything was done to get a fan base

Arizona coach Lute Olson gives Steve Kerr instruction. Kerr helped the determined Olson revitalize the UA program and its fan base.

going. They'd play in front of hundreds and sometimes a thousand fans.

"Lute was smart," said Kerr. "He was trying to get interest throughout the state with intrasquad games. It was fun. We had a good time. It also shows you just how far the program has come."

WANT A TICKET?

During Kerr's freshman year—Olson's first—he was at the 7-11 convenience store and had tickets to a game.

"I had the tickets in my pocket," Kerr recalled. "I wanted to give them to people, but they said thanks, but that they couldn't go. Now, tickets are like gold."

THE OPENER

The Lute Olson era opened the regular season against Northern Arizona at home in McKale Center on November 25, 1983. There was a whopping 3,000 fans in attendance. UA's coaches were shocked.

"Lute and I looked at each other (wondering what was going on)," said Thompson. "We could have shot off a cannon in there and not hit anyone. We rolled our eyes and couldn't believe it."

The two then turned to assistant Ricky Byrdsong, who was the lone coaching holdover from the Lindsey era. "What do you do when you have recruits in town?" they asked. "Don't say you subject them to this—poor fan support and indifference," they added.

"Well," Thompson said of Byrdsong's reply, "we take them to the hockey games at the convention center to see some enthusiasm."

Arizona won the game, 72-65.

LOSING THEIR WAY

If anyone questioned Olson's passion for the game, it came early in his UA coaching career. After beating NAU to begin the season, it was downhill from there. Arizona didn't win another game for more than a month, losing six straight. But it was that 65-60 loss to Pan American that got some of the players' juices going, seeing in part the desire of Olson to win.

"I remember Lute shattering a clipboard against the wall," said Kerr. "He was embarrassed and angry. But we just weren't good."

Pete Williams recalled that the clipboard almost hit him, remembering Olson saying, "'I see why you were a bunch of losers last year.' Lute just walked out of the locker room after that."

TO TEXAS OR BUST

It took Arizona going 1-6 in the early part of Olson's first season to start playing better. And it took a trip to the Sun Bowl Tournament in El Paso, Texas, to get the Wildcats going.

Arizona was in the same tournament as ranked Michigan, a good Texas Tech team and host UTEP. In the opener, UA stunned Texas Tech, beating the Red Raiders 51-49 to get a chance to play host Miners.

Arizona gave the Miners everything they could handle and more in the title game, eventually losing 51-49 in overtime. UA had a chance to win it at the buzzer, but Brock Brunkhorst's 30-footer missed.

Olson was irate, feeling his team was given a hometown job by the referees.

"I think the most valuable player trophy should go to (referee) Walt Reynolds," Olson said after the game. "He really earned it. They can say what they want as to what team won, but we won the basketball game. There was no way he (Reynolds) was going to let us win."

Even famed UTEP coach Don Haskins said he felt UA won.

"That was a game where I actually cried after the game," said Pete Williams. "If you looked at where the program was the year before and where we were and how we played in that tournament with Michigan, UTEP and Texas Tech, you could understand. We went out there and outplayed those guys. And had we won (that UTEP game) that would have been a shocker. I cried because we came so close.

"But that game also showed we could play and compete and win. It took a while, but we got it going."

BREAKTHROUGH GAME

Two days after Steve Kerr's father was assassinated in 1984, UA played Arizona State, a team dominating the series until then, winning nine straight. But behind an emotional Wildcat team, UA made it a rout.

"We just crushed them," said Kerr. "That was a big win. And to me that's when people really started to show interest and show signs that, yes, this could be a good program."

Said Pete Williams: "We destroyed them; it was awesome. It was a good feeling considering how much they had dominated UA in the past. Sure, it was nice to sweep UCLA, but ASU? That was even better and it continued after I left."

It was UA's first sweep of ASU since 1970.

Arizona eventually went 5-4 the second half of the regular season, including a win against a tough Oregon State team.

IT'S UA AT THE BUZZER

In beating the Sun Devils for a sweep of the season series in 1984, guard Eddie Smith was the reason.

On that night on February 17, 1984, Smith's shot that bounced around the rim fell through with no time left on the clock.

"It's a bitch," ASU coach Bob Weinhaur said then.

Just 11 months later, again in Tempe, Smith proved to be the hero in knocking off ASU for the second time in dramatic fashion. He hit an unbelievable scoop shot and a free throw to give UA a 61-60 come-from-behind win. ASU had a 60-53 lead with 37 seconds left, but behind Smith UA came back. It was his dramatic basket over Bobby Thompson that proved to UA fans it was destiny in that it was a near-impossible shot.

Smith scored and was fouled with 26 seconds left to close the gap to 60-56. After Thompson missed the front end of a one and one, Morgan Taylor hit a 20-foot jumper to make it 60-58 with nine seconds left.

But as ASU attempted to inbound the ball, Pete Williams deflected the pass, and in the scramble, Smith picked up the ball and raced toward the basket. But Thompson hammered Smith as he just barely was able to release the ball—for the tie and the eventual winning free throw.

THE SELLOUT

It took just over a season and a half before Arizona finally got its first sellout crowd in the Olson era. It came against always-tough Oregon State on February 23, 1985. The previous sell-out came in 1980 when UA faced then NCAA runner-up UCLA.

"I remember the game being on TV, too," said Williams. "It was a bit eery because Lute was just saying this was a great spot for college basketball. There were a bunch of fans yelling behind him (after the game while on TV). I think it's even exceeded his expectations. It was just incredible."

It was also a game that still remains one of Arizona's best, hitting 71 percent (25 of 35) of its field goals. It's a school record for a game.

WILLIAMS OUT OF BOUNDS

Just two years removed from being a laughingstock in the Pac-10, Arizona was on the verge of winning the conference before heading to Washington and UCLA in late February and early March. But two things happened: UA lost to Washington in Marv Harshman's final home game in Seattle and then a group of UA players (Pete Williams and Morgan Taylor included) were out late after the game, resulting in a team suspension for the next game against UCLA.

"I use that as an example when I talk to people," said Williams, now a probation officer. "I say nobody is bigger than the program, and that if you screw up you have to live with the consequences. I use what I did as an example. There are no guarantees we would have beaten UCLA (for the title) but I regret it and have for much of my life. You just never know."

It came about after UA players went out after losing 60–58 to UW. At the time, UA had won eight of nine conference games and was in the hunt for its first Pac-10 title. As it turned out, Washington and USC shared the league crown as each finished 13-5. Oregon State, UA and UCLA tied for third at 13-6.

"We got jobbed at Washington," said Williams. "I'm not one to make excuses, but we were jobbed. It was Harshman's final home game. We were pissed so we went out."

They went out too late, returning to the hotel way into the morning hours. They were caught and suspended.

"Coach (Olson) didn't say a word to me from the time we left Washington to the time we got to Los Angeles," Williams said. "The only thing he did say was at practice. He told me to turn my jersey to the opposite color (practice team)."

After practice, Olson gathered the team and asked the players who were out why they'd do such a thing. "Some of the guys gave lame excuses," Williams said. "As soon as it got around to me and my explanation, Coach just looked straight down to the ground ... talk about disappointment. That just sliced me. He wouldn't even look at me. It's one of the biggest regrets I have."

Arizona proceeded to lose 58-54 to the Bruins.

UA TITLE HOLDERS

Arizona finally had arrived, beating king of the conference UCLA 88-76 on March 3, 1986.

It also marked the first time UA had beaten the Bruins in Westwood since 1923. In a game of future stars, Arizona's Sean Elliott outdid UCLA's Reggie Miller, a one-time recruit of UA. Elliott had 28 points.

"It was great because Reggie Miller was talking so much stuff," said John Edgar. "We just wanted to beat them so bad. It was great to be part of that atmosphere. But Reggie being Reggie, he said, 'You won this one, but I'm going to be in the NBA.'"

Nothing, however, could put a damper on Arizona's meteoric rise to the top, just two seasons before Arizona had won only one conference game. And in beating the Bruins that March day, UA had swept the season series over the Bruins for the first time in school history.

"That was one of my most memorable games with UA just because of my past with UCLA," said Kerr, who was a ball boy and a fan of the Bruins in his younger years. "We had an incredible second half. We shot 15 of 20 and just overtook them. We flew back on the charter and everyone was so excited. We had the greatest time on the plane coming back home."

AUTOGRAPH, PLEASE

Shortly after UA had defeated the Bruins in Pauley Pavilion, Bobbi Olson, Lute's longtime wife, sauntered up to former UCLA legendary coach John Wooden asking if he'd autograph that day's game program—just for old-times' sake and for the Olson family.

After all, Lute Olson has long thought of Wooden as his mentor, the model of consistency and success when it came to college basketball.

"We still have the program at home," Lute said. "I've been asked a number of times, 'Why do you have a program from UCLA on the wall?' Well, it was sort of the changing of the guard. Having been in Southern California (as a high school and college coach) and following the success of the Bruins, for us to go in there and win—in a year when we were picked to finish eighth—was nice."

Even at 93 years of age, Wooden remembered the incident that occurred in 1986.

"I've known Lute and Bobbi through the years," Wooden said. "They have been very dear to me, not just as a coach, but as people. Bobbi, whenever they played UCLA, came by and gave me a hug."

'BAMA SLAMMA

Nearly a decade after making the NCAA tournament and two years removed from Olson being hired, Arizona was back in the NCAA tournament. UA finished the regular season in 1985 with a respectable record at 21-9 and in a tie for third place in Pac-10 play.

"We all went to one of the booster's houses to watch the show," Williams recalled of the NCAA pairings. "It was an exciting time. We thought we were in."

Then it showed that No. 10 seed Arizona was to face No. 7 seed Alabama in the first round in Albuquerque.

"Once they showed that I said, 'Bobby Lee Hurt and Derrick McKey,'" said Williams, referring to two Crimson Tide players.

Arizona lost 50-41.

"It was tough on the seniors, because it was their last game," said Kerr. "But we looked at it as a great experience."

A Character

When a little-known center signed with Arizona in 1984, little did anyone know how much fun he'd provide. And not all the fun and excitement was exclusive to the basketball floor.

Joe Turner, a six-foot-nine center/forward, proved to be one of Arizona's all-time funniest characters—if not one of the most loved. Yet, most of the admiration came because he was fun loving and carefree.

"He was a great guy to be around," Olson said. "He had a tremendous effect on helping us recruit. He was fun and personable."

And although his nickname was "Little Joe" because his father was "Big Joe," Olson called him Little Pete "because he always followed Pete (Williams) around."

Yet, what Turner is most known for is his way with words —sort of. He was Arizona's version of Yogi Berra.

"Once there was a couple in an elevator and he got in and said, 'I'll bet I know what floor you're on.'" Olson said, in telling the story. "They said, 'What floor?'

"'Six,' Turner replied.

"'How did you know?' the couple said.

"'Because I have ESPN,' Turner said, seriously."

MORE TURNER

Turner was the king of the malapropism. Here are a few ditties:

One day while some of UA's players were watching a game, an announcer asked, "Where is UAB?

Turner quickly said, "UA be in Tucson." His teammates cracked up because the announcer meant UAB as in University of Alabama-Birmingham.

Another moment came when the team was having dinner and there was a decision to be made. After the waitress finished with the choices—one being the soup or salad—he said that sounded good, so he'd take the "super salad."

Yes, there's more.

As is typical in Arizona's season, it plays in an exhibition game or two before the regular season starts. Such was the case in 1987 when the Soviet National team came to Tucson for a game.

Turner wasn't worried, in part because it was only "an expedition" game and they don't count against the overall win-loss record.

There was the time during the football season when the players were watching a game that started a debate about who would win the Heisman Trophy. There was no doubt about it, according to Turner.

"Vinny Tankaverde will win it hands down," he said.

Of course, he meant Vinny Testaverde of Miami, Florida.

"He's one of my all-time favorite people," Kerr said. "He's always smiling and fun to be around. He was just a great teammate, keeping everyone loose."

John Edger said Turner could do no wrong at UA.

"People think he's goofy," said Edgar, "but he's a smart dude, one smart guy."

He's still perhaps one of the most popular players to ever play in the Lute Olson era.

"The guy is never down," said Williams. "He knew everybody on campus. Either that or they knew him. Here he was with this big 'ol Kool-Aid smile—from ear to ear. He'd say hello to everybody. That was just his personality."

CHALKBOARD TALK

Turner being Turner found himself in a tough spot after a 59-58 loss against New Mexico in 1984. It was the second consecutive loss after UA had won seven straight wins to open the season.

"Joe blew an assignment," Williams recalled. "So Lute made him go up to the chalkboard and show us what we were supposed to do."

Turner obliged. But in the process it became one of the funnier moments for Williams. Here was this massive chalkboard, and Turner proceeded to draw a basketball key no bigger than two inches where it could hardly be seen from a distance.

While up there Turner looked around, wondering what should have happened, but Olson quickly said, "Don't look for help," in figuring out what went wrong.

"We left the locker room just falling out laughing," Williams said. "And you know that Coach Olson just wanted to scream."

BON VOYAGE

After the 1984-85 season, UA went on its European Tour, where it would play 15 games in 17 days. They went from Yugoslavia to France to Spain to Italy and parts in between. Upon arriving in Amsterdam, UA players were surprised at what they saw.

"It was my first experience in a red-light district," said Williams. "We were just amazed. I didn't know what all that was about."

If nudity and the like seemed out of the ordinary for Wildcat players, so did the public drinking.

"We'd go to a restaurant or pub and they'd put stuff in our drink," said Edgar. "I didn't know what it was."

The Cats saw a number of sites, visiting the Eiffel Tower in Paris; windmills in the Netherlands; and much more. But one of the most imposing figures was Arvydas Sabonis, the seven-foot-three, 270-pound Russian who at the time was just a 21-year-old phenom and perhaps one of Europe's best players. Three years later, he'd lead the Russians to a gold medal in the Seoul Olympics.

"It was incredible," said Williams. "We had Joe Turner (six foot nine, 195 pounds) and he just dwarfed Joe. He made Joe look like he was this big (placing his thumb and forefinger about an inch apart)."

KING GUMBY

Bruce Fraser wasn't green but one of the guys who made Arizona basketball very good in the mid-1980s. Good because everyone knew their roles. Fraser was one who knew his spot on the team and didn't complain much about little playing time. Olson's first few years were built on having players like Fraser.

Early in Fraser's career he came up with the phrase "Gumby," the green cartoon character that was stiff and mostly immobile.

"I came up with it, because when I'd eventually get in the game after sitting on the bench I was always tight," Fraser said. "I'd be put into the games with just a few minutes left. Coming from a successful high school program, that was tough. It was hard coming into a game tight."

But he and many others did. One game, Fraser decided to place a three-inch Gumby figurine in his sock for some symbolism and/or good luck.

One game—one he was fortunate to play in—it popped out of his sock.

"The ref saw it and picked it up. He was like, 'What's this?'" Fraser said.

Fraser quickly claimed it.

"Steve Kerr was the only one who knew I had it in my sock," Fraser said. "Usually the only time I got in was when we were up 20 points."

A year later, when Fraser became a grad assistant, the Gumby legend grew. More bench players, claimed to be Gumbies and were proud of it.

"These guys were all vocal and energetic," said Fraser. "They were some good players, but there were so many guys in front of them."

Yet, being a Gumby wasn't easy.

"They were all good players but they sat on the bench, so that was tough," Fraser said. "Everybody felt they should play more and probably should have. Your ego takes over. Your pride hurts when you're on that bench."

But Olson appreciated all of them. In fact, he said, it was a key to the program in the early years.

"I've said many times that the key to a program is when you talk to the 12th man, and he's sold on the program," Olson said. "That's what the Gumbies were. Even though they weren't getting much time, they were a key for us in practice. They had great attitudes, and the fans saw that, game in and game out. It was an unusual situation."

CAR TROUBLE

On a trip back to school, Tom Tolbert began to have car trouble. It was just outside of the California border, but luckily teammate Craig McMillan was following him.

"Tolbert said it made some inhuman noise, something he had never heard before," Fraser said. "It basically just died on him. So he coasted to the side of the road where it just stopped."

Tolbert being Tolbert—an off-the-wall character—proceeded to take everything he could out of his Ford Mercury and put it in McMillan's car.

"Whatever he couldn't take he just left," Fraser said. "Then out of frustration he took a baseball bat he had in the car and started teeing off on it. He destroyed the emblem on the front, eventually breaking out the lights and windows. One of the last things he did was put his Arizona basketball shoes on top of the hood."

He must have forgotten them. A couple of days later a few of the other basketball players who lived in California passed through the same spot Tolbert left his car.

"We knew that was Tolbert's car," Fraser said. "The shoes were still there. I thought he'd be there, too. But he wasn't."

Tom Tolbert, forward-center, could get offensive a time or two.

LOFTON COMMITS TO UA

One of the best athletes and perhaps the best athlete in Olson's early years at Arizona was Kenny Lofton, a five-foot-10 guard from Washington High in East Chicago, Indiana.

He committed to Arizona after waking up at 3 a.m. one morning, deciding UA was the place to be.

In commenting about Lofton, Olson said, "He's quick and a great leaper."

That may have been an understatement. While on the recruiting trip, when UA players couldn't believe Lofton could do a 360-degree dunk, Lofton did just that, proving he could.

UA players were amazed.

"Everyone knows the guys who come in are good, but he was so athletic," Fraser said. "He was raw, and his game wasn't defined. He had a tough time adjusting to Coach's system. It wasn't what he was used to."

But after some struggle, Lofton adjusted.

"His game evolved—everybody's does," Fraser said. "Kenny's more than others.

"But Kenny was the most athletic player I had ever been around. And we had Sean Elliott and Harvey Mason. Kenny was such an incredible athlete."

Whether Lofton was running wind sprints or going through biometric workouts, "Kenny was so far ahead of everyone, it was crazy," Fraser said. "In strength and agility drills, he just killed it. He's a guy who could have played pro football or basketball or baseball."

Lofton eventually received a multiyear contract playing pro baseball, gaining all-star status midway through his career.

"Part of the thing that was tough on him was that he followed Steve Kerr at the point guard spot," Fraser said. "It's like the guy who is going to follow Lute Olson. Unless you do better, it's going to be tough. Following Steve Kerr in Tucson at that point in time? Come on. Kenny wasn't that type of player. He'd make mistakes, but he'd also give you some high-lights. Maybe if he was in a different system or had he played early on, he might have played in the NBA."

SHOE BUSINESS

On one trip, UA assistant coach Byrdsong, now deceased, for-got to pack his dress shoes. He didn't realize it until just before the team was ready to head to the game, so he asked booster George Kalil if he could borrow his shoes. They had to be big enough. Well, they were too big. Kalil wears a size 16. But being that it was so late to go shopping, Byrdsong wore them anyway.

"They're just too big for him," Thompson said. "But he wore them all night."

And he looked like Bozo the Clown.

Chapter 5

1987-88
FINAL FOUR

SOMETHING SPECIAL TO HAPPEN

It was early November of 1987, and the annual Red-Blue game was set to be played. There was more hype going into the season than any previous season under Lute Olson.

There was a big crowd at McKale Center hoping to get a glimpse of their Cats. Arizona would eventually be ranked No. 17 in the Associated Press poll; No. 10 in the UPI poll to begin the season. But even before the polls were out, the players knew it was going to be a special season.

"Coming in as a freshmen I didn't have any idea how loved Steve Kerr was in Tucson," Muehlebach said. "And in classic Steve Kerr form, he hits his first shot in the Red-Blue game. Of course, as we all know now that's what Steve does. But after that night I could just feel something special was going to happen that year."

Arizona eventually set a school record by going 35-3, playing in its first Final Four.

IOWA BOUND—AND GAGGED

The day before Arizona was to play Iowa, UA had had a horrible practice. UA seemed destined to lose.

"Lute was worried, and we were all worried," said Kerr.

Then the tip-off came, and Arizona was en route to the win.

"We didn't turn the ball over much; we were kind of methodical," said Kerr. "It was one of those games where everything went well, and one of those games early on where we were pretty good."

The nerves in practice were obvious. After all, Olson was back in his old stomping grounds—Iowa. Just seven years earlier he had taken the Hawkeyes to the Final Four and just five years prior was still the Hawkeyes coach.

Then he moved to Arizona.

When Arizona went to Iowa it had all the makings of a made-for-TV event. Olson was back. And he was amazingly still very much loved there.

"He was so nervous," said Steve Kerr. "It was amazing to see him walk onto the floor. The crowd went crazy. It seemed like the head of state walked into the building. Lute always has had a commanding presence, but he was walking into an arena with his own people. It was pretty impressive."

Arizona, undefeated at 6-0, was ranked No. 4 in the nation. Iowa was No. 3.

And at the time, Olson publicly said, "You don't spend nine years of your life in a place where you know all those people and have all those great memories without coming back feeling a special kind of feeling."

What helped was Arizona won, 66-59, giving Olson one of his most memorable victories.

"It was tough going back," Olson said. "We had been involved in raising money for the new facility, and everyone in there was a fan throughout the time I was there.

"It was probably as pressure-packed a situation as I've ever been involved in. We had a lot of friends there with a lot of people making the program what it was. That's what made it tough. After the game, a lot of the friends said let's not do that one again. It was difficult for everyone."

A week later, Arizona became the No. 1 team in the nation for the first time.

No. 1—and Proud

After disposing of Iowa, Arkansas-Little Rock and Washington, Arizona stretched its record to 9-0 for the first part of the 1987-88 season.

Then came the Associated Press poll on December 21, 1987 where Arizona was ranked No. 1 for the first time in school history.

"That was cool," said Kerr. "We were all excited."

And with reason. No one was coming close to Arizona, particularly after winning the Great Alaska Shootout just a month prior. UA started the season ranked No. 17.

"It was a sign that we had arrived," said Olson. "We had played a tough schedule that second year and got beat by a number of Big 10 schools, so we were not there yet. Then we won the tournament (Great Alaska Shootout), and that sort of opened everyone's eyes to us."

Drug Test Him

What is Lute Olson like? After four and a half years of that constant question, Kerr had had enough. He then came up with one of his famous one-liners.

It was during his senior year and during the Fiesta Bowl Classic—the best anyone can remember—when he said, "Despite his heroin addiction, he's doing well for himself."

As Olson said then and he says now, "Only one person could get away with saying that, and that was Steve."

Known for his quick humor, Kerr had given a great quote about his straight-and-narrow coach.

"I think I shocked some people with that one," Kerr said. "There were a few laughs and a few gasps. But people who knew it was so farfetched with Lute that people understood the humor of it. ... I hope, anyway."

S-CAR-GO

On road trips UA typically eats at some of the best restaurants in the best cities. In Sean Rooks's first season—his redshirt freshman year—the team was out at dinner and Rooks saw something he thought might be good. It was escargot.

"We were all spoiled," Bruce Fraser said. "Some of the guys (if not all of them) were lucky to be in restaurants like the ones we were in. Then some would complain if the lobster wasn't right."

Rooks had his eye on the escargot.

"What's es–car–got?" Rooks said. "Sean Elliott says, 'You should order that—it's good. Order it.'"

Heck, Rooks couldn't even pronounce it.

When the order arrived it was what it was—snails.

"Snails?" Rooks said, "I didn't order snails."

He just grimaced, Fraser said of Rooks's reaction. He didn't eat one.

MUSIC MAN

Arizona was "Wild about the Cats" in 1988. And that was on the court, off the court and on the radio waves. Everyone can thank junior Harvey Mason, a talented guard who had a long background in music.

His father is Harvey Mason, Sr., an established composer, musician and producer.

It must have been in the genes.

As Arizona was having its most glorious season and was headed to the school's first Final Four, Mason decided to write a song about the Cats. The idea came about between KRQQ disc jockey Mike Elliott and Mason.

"I did it in one night," Mason said. "It was great just hanging with all the guys. It was incredible."

Indeed.

Once it hit the airwaves—exclusively on KRQQ (93.7)—it was a smash hit. The players sang their lyrics, and it was a catchy rap tune.

Some lyrics included:

★ "I'll drill it in from three-point land," Steve Kerr sang.

★ "Give me the ball and stand back and watch me jam for two," Anthony Cook bellowed.

★ "I'd better find the open man and get the ball down low," Craig McMillan said.

It was just a fun time for UA, then the No. 2-ranked team in the country.

"It was just a special time, because most of us were over-achievers," said reserve Bruce Fraser. "The town went crazy for it. The city took to us, and one of those connections was that song. And it brought the team closer in another way. Harvey was the instrumental guy with that."

It took two weeks to record, as they sat in someone's garage and did their individual recordings.

"He put us through a lot," Fraser said. "I knew he was talented but he produced it. He had everything laid out. It was just fun. No one expected it to take off. It was No. 1 on the charts."

UA VS. SMART GUYS

After finishing the 1988 regular season with a school-record 31-2 during the regular season, Arizona was prepared for anything as it looked toward the NCAA tournament.

When the bracket came out that Selection Sunday, it was no surprise Arizona was given the No. 1 seed in the West, having to play Cornell in the first round of the tournament.

Upon looking at the bracket, Kerr said it would be like "playing five Steve Kerrs."

He added later, "You can't win with five of them. You can only have one (Steve Kerr)."

Arizona won 90-50.

It was still a tough road, because UA's experience in the postseason hadn't been kind the previous three years, having gone 0-fer in first-round games.

"We (as a team) hadn't won an NCAA tournament game until then (Cornell), but we knew we were in a good position to make a big run for the first time," Kerr said. "The previous years we thought we could win one or two games, but this year we knew we were there. We had a shot to go all the way."

Seton Hauled Out

Despite Arizona being the No. 1 seed in the West, there still were doubts about just how good the Wildcats were. Perhaps vulnerable?

At least some TV commentators felt so.

"We were watching TV, and everyone was saying we could lose," Kerr recalled. "Jim Nantz and Billy Packer and some others on TV were saying look for Seton Hall to possibly upset Arizona. We were definitely threatened.

"But we crushed them, too," Kerr said.

Arizona moved on to the Sweet 16 with an 84-55 victory.

Heading to Final Four

Arizona had just beaten North Carolina in Seattle and was now headed to Kansas City for the 1988 Final Four. What's a team to do as it rode a high never reached before in the history of Arizona basketball?

Well, go after its coach's impeccable hair.

"We all ganged up on him," Mason said. "We wanted to see if it was real. We were rubbing it so hard that I'm sure it hurt his head. We figured it had to be a wig because it never moved. It looked like a helmet. We roughed him up."

Most know that Bennett Davison mussed Olson's hair, after UA won the national title game in 1977

"And whatever Bennett did was minor to what we did," said Matt Muehlebach. "But whatever Lute does to that hair it's almost impossible to mess it up."

Muhlebach said Davison was just one guy going at Olson's hair in 1997 when UA won the title, "we had 15 hands in there just trying to mess it up."

How did he react?

"He loved it," he said. "But when we stepped back, in two seconds it just returned to what it was."

The Kiss and Hug

It's one of the more memorable moments of the 1988 NCAA tournament. Arizona gets by North Carolina in a rout and Bobbi races down to the Kingdome court to give her husband a celebratory kiss and hug. They were back at the Final Four for the first time since 1980 when they were with Iowa.

"I was surprised to see her; it was all spontaneous," Olson said. "It definitely had an effect on recruiting, because there were a lot of mothers that saw the involvement of Bobbi in the program."

Not So OK

Kerr remembers it like it was yesterday. After all, one doesn't forget one of their worst performances in history. With Arizona rolling right along in the NCAA tournament—a big reason was Kerr's shooting—the Wildcats had every reason to believe they'd make it to the NCAA title game.

But it wasn't to be, particularly in light of Kerr, the nation's best outside shooter, going two for 13 from the floor, easily his worst game of the season.

"I still think about it," Kerr said. "Maybe I'm a pathetic loser and I need to let it go, but even 16 years later I still think about that game. It's without question—second is not even close—the most difficult game I've ever played in and still the most difficult result to handle."

Part—if not most—of the hurt comes from feeling Arizona had the best team in the tournament. Sure Oklahoma, Kansas and Duke were tough, but they were hardly on a roll compared to Arizona. Yet, Arizona fell to the Sooners, 86-78.

"I know deep down that all I had to do is play the way I normally do and just make some shots," said Kerr. "I had three or four shots early in the game that just rattled in and out, but they felt perfect. I just got into a rut. I could never get into a rhythm. I guess the pressure of the Final Four got to me. I definitely started to press. I just couldn't find a groove."

Some thought that Kerr might have pressed because his mom, Anne, was in the stands watching. Not coincidentally, he had a poor game against Stanford when she was also in attendance, which was a rare occurrence.

"I really never gave it that much thought," Kerr said, of playing in front of his beloved mom. "My mom never put any pressure on me. She just supports me. Maybe (the pressure) was self-imposed, but I never thought about it."

Going in, Kerr thought he'd have a great game. He didn't feel good about his teammates, who couldn't hit anything during practice at Kemper Arena.

Then came the game. It was miserable.

"I hit shots in warmups and I felt great, couldn't have felt better going into a game," Kerr said. "I was playing with more confidence than I had ever had. Then it all went wrong."

He missed his first one from the corner and it snowballed into failure.

"Everything was just an inch too long, but the shot was dead on line, just too long," he said. "I guess my adrenaline may have been too high."

Lute Gets Emotional

Rare is the time when Olson gets emotional, perhaps just a handful of times. Losing to Oklahoma at the Final Four was one of those times.

"Everybody was emotional, and there probably wasn't a dry eye in the locker room," said Muehlebach. "It was one of those things where we were upset we lost. It was such a perfect season. We had such incredible chemistry and the closeness of that team was unbelievable. Things like that don't happen often. It was an incredible year."

Muehlebach called the season a feel-good movie. And Arizona and all its players were the stars.

"There was no other ending but to win it all," he said. "So it was surprising on one hand, but shocking in that the season was over and we couldn't believe it."

Someone even thought they saw a tear in Olson's eye. It was that devastating.

"It was a real difficult time," Olson said. "That was a team that should have won it. What was difficult for me was that it was the group that put Arizona basketball on the map. It was the team that had the first No. 1 ranking. There were seniors Tom Tolbert, Steve Kerr and Craig McMillan. It was such a sad ending ... a very difficult time."

A Time to Remember

In all, it was a glorious year for Arizona in 1987-88. UA finished at a school-best 35-3, losing only twice in the regular season and then finally to Oklahoma in the school's first Final Four.

The run brought the city together for one purpose—to cheer on the Cats.

"It was magical," said Kerr. "All the stars were aligned for that season. I returned from an injury, and the team was so well balanced. Everybody had matured to become real good players. Everybody played roles. And the chemistry was just perfect."

Chapter 6

LATE 1980s

HAPPY THANKSGIVING

The Wildcats were on the road to begin the 1988 season in Alaska at a time when it's about family and friends. It was Thanksgiving.

UA decided to get the players host families, where they'd spend time with family hosts who would treat the players to a good, warm meal.

Among those paired up were Jud Buechler and Harvey Mason. Sean Elliott and Kenny Lofton.

"Kenny and Sean went to a house where the mom and dad picked them up ... and they went to Sizzler," Mason said. "It was the most horrible thing ever. Classic."

On that same trip, Sean Rooks joined a family and they took him to their home.

"Obviously, we're in Alaska, and we're in the wilderness," Rooks said. "I'm watching TV and off to my left I see something move from the corner of my eye. I see the whole background of the window shift. It drew my eye. When I looked up there was a moose. It was just there walking around in the backyard. Unbelievable."

ORANGE YOU NICE

While on the recruiting trail, assistant coach Kevin O'Neill and former UA assistant Ken Burmeister ran into each other while recruiting. Same hotel, some hotel bar. Burmeister was the head coach at Texas-San Antonio, but in order for Burmeister to save money, Burmeister stayed with O'Neill.

"Burmeister was still out looking at kids, and O'Neill came back early so he went down to the bar and had a couple of beers," Fraser said.

But then O'Neill being O'Neill—fun, strange, different— he went back to the room and got every orange shirt (his team's colors) that Burmeister had and gave them to the people in the bar."

Later in the night when Burmeister met O'Neill in the bar he got an orange surprise.

"Everyone was wearing his stuff," Fraser said. "Burmeister laughed, but he was upset."

ROAD CREW DUO

To earn money during the summer months, Southern Californians Fraser and Anthony Cook worked on roads and interstates. It was good money, but the heat was scorching.

"Anthony told me that was the first time he had never seen me smile," Fraser said. "That was tough work. You're talking 110 degrees. Here you are in Needles, California, on the highway."

Cook wasn't smiling either.

"He was a hard worker. I have to give it to him for that," Fraser said.

"A.C. worked every road crew because he wanted to make as much money as he could."

Then came the night he worked a double shift and it turned out he lost money.

"We worked in LA in the morning and then somewhere else later," Fraser said. "He had just bought an expensive pair of boots. We went to take a two-hour nap then went back only to find his brand-new boots smoldering in a fire that had started. There were right there, crispy and black in the construction yard."

KERR GONE, OTHICK IN

A season after golden boy Steve Kerr graduated from Arizona, another blond, sharp-shooting guard entered the program. He was six-foot-two Matt Othick, a point guard/shooting guard who reminded many—fairly or unfairly—of favorite son Kerr.

"I never did like it," Othick said of the label. "I never played like Steve. Yes, we were both 6-2, 6-3 guards, but I was flashier. I came from Vegas. I was more of a playmaker than a shooter. I got molded into a player like Steve Kerr as I went through it."

Othick lived with the label of being like Steve Kerr for four years.

"I respected Steve Kerr and thought he was a great player," Othick said. "But I hated it when people said I was the next Steve Kerr. I didn't feel that I had to live up to it. I didn't want the label, but it wasn't like it was the worst thing in the world as a player."

In the Can

Assistant coach Kevin O'Neill was one of the more outspoken, opinionated people in the last 20 years at Arizona. He spoke his mind.

One night he went too far with then-graduate assistant Craig McMillan in the middle of the 1989 NCAA tournament.

The day before Arizona was to play Clemson in the Sweet 16, O'Neill, McMillan, Fraser and others went out for St. Patrick's Day. Upon returning to their hotel late in the night, McMillan and O'Neill got into a heated debate "about some play on *SportsCenter*" as Fraser remembered it.

It came on the heels of nearly getting into a fight with patrons at a bar where opposing fans were criticizing Olson.

O'Neill and McMillan's argument was so loud hotel officials called the cops, who came for the two.

They were taken away in handcuffs "and the two are still fighting about something," Fraser said.

"Coach calls me later to say he heard something about the guys being noisy, but I told him everything was OK and that it was the guys next to us," Fraser said. "But I'm freaking out because they're both in jail."

The two were bailed out early in the morning. Olson knew of their plight. One of the first things Olson said as O'Neill got on the bus was, "You better pray that we win."

Arizona did, beating Clemson 94-68.

"We were so good, we beat Clemson pretty handily," Fraser said.

KODAK MOMENT

No question Olson is a very private person. And especially when it comes to his appearance. But on the team's European trip, the guys got a rare glimpse of their coach.

"He'd never show his body when he was around the players," Othick said.

"We'd always laugh because he'd never get undressed in front of us."

Except one time at Washington State when they didn't have time to get to the hotel after the game.

"Every guy was eyeballing him," Othick said. "He was so uncomfortable.

"He hid behind something and got dressed. It was funny."

Then came the time in Europe.

"He has always had this perfect hair and he was always dressed perfectly," Othick said. "We're out with all the guys walking on the beach when who do we see on the beach? It's Lute and Bobbi. Lute is out there like a beached whale, it was during his heavier days (he laughs).

"Ron (Curry) had a camera, so he took the picture."

Curry already had decided he was transferring, so he wasn't afraid to take the picture.

"Lute knew we got him," Othick said. "I laughed so hard."

McWILDERBEAST

Legend has it Craig McMillan predicted an earthquake in Alaska. He's such an outdoorsman his teammates nicknamed him McWilderbeast for his penchant to be outdoors.

Muehlebach says he's Brad Pitt's character in the movie *Legends of the Fall*.

"He's part animal, part man," Muehlebach said. "He's an incredible outdoorsman. He loves being outdoors. One time when we missed a flight in Seattle and were stranded, he eventually slept on the airport floor."

Othick recalled the time when the team went on a European tour and some players were looking for some cliffs to dive off of.

"We sent McMillan to scout out a spot for us," Othick said. "One time he goes down to the edge of the rocks and jumps off, going to the bottom of the water. He comes back and was dead calm."

The players asked how it was and what happened.

"All of a sudden he shows us this type of sea creature on his foot," Othick said. "There were huge needles. He was walking with a limp, but it didn't bother him. I would have been panicked."

THE PREDICTION

It was 1989 and the team was in Southern California for a game. As was usual, Arizona stayed close to the Santa Monica beach. The day before a game, while Othick, Sean Rooks and Wayne Womack took a walk on the beach Othick said, "Wouldn't it be cool if an earthquake hit?"

"I was being this cocky little idiot," Othick said. "They both looked at me like I was completely nuts."

They figured what did Othick know of earthquakes being that he's from Las Vegas and they were from Southern California? They'd been through earthquakes and it's not fun.

"They got rattled," Othick said.

Three hours later an earthquake hit.

"I'm there running around like a little baby," Othick said. "It was the scariest thing I've ever been in. I was like a little

Whether he was outplaying Shaquille O'Neal or rescuing Craig McMillan from a broken elevator, Sean Rooks looked like Superman to his teammates. (Ken Levine/Getty Images)

kid looking for Rooks to help me. It was the most bizarre thing."

BET YOU WON'T

Arizona stays at the Valley River Inn when it makes its annual annual trip to Oregon. The hotel sits on the bank of the Williamette River.

One time, the team bet Craig McMillan would not go into the water.

"We pitched in money and dared him to do it," said Sean Rooks. "That water was flowing that night. It was moving. He gets into it and loses his balance, but he did it. McMillan was the craziest."

And sometimes the wimpiest.

Rooks said while on the team's trip to Europe in 1989, there were about eight UA players in an old elevator—a lift—at the team's hotel. It was only built for four people, but they didn't realize it until it was too late.

"Four personas, 280 kg. Max," the sign read.

"I saw at least four guys who were 280 kilograms each," Harvey Mason said.

As the elevator started to move it also began making a horrible noise.

"We were obviously too much weight. It stopped between floors and we got stuck," Rooks said. "They didn't have the technology that we have. We tried to open the doors, but after about three or four minutes we knew we were stuck."

In the meantime, everyone panicked. Othick thought they'd run out of air. And McMillan just freaked out, letting out a noise, Mason said, that could be heard in Tucson.

"This is the same guy who cliff dives and swims in a river," Rooks said.

"He shrieks to the top of his lungs, 'You got to get me out of here.' I grabbed the door, pushed and jolted it open and climbed out."

Mason and the rest couldn't believe it.

"Rooks was like Superman," Mason said. "We all shimmied out one at a time. It must have looked like something out of the circus with all the clowns piling out of a small car."

GET CLOTHES, PLEASE

Brian Williams was from Las Vegas, and so was Othick. So why not become roommates as teammates at Arizona? Right? Well, Othick saw plenty when it came to Williams, a six-foot-11 center/forward for Arizona.

One day he saw too much, although it was widely known Williams, an eccentric, loved to be in the buff.

While living together at a Tucson apartment during Othick's freshman year, Othick saw Williams in all his glory.

After the two returned from a early-morning run with the team, Williams decided to take a dip in the pool to get refreshed.

"We got back from the run and he was in front of the window with only his basketball shoes on—he was naked in the window," Othick said, adding that the main office was right in front of their apartment. "There were all these cars coming in and out. I couldn't take it. He asked if I wanted to go for a swim, but I wasn't going if he was going out like that."

Williams didn't. He took a towel.

"But he took a towel that fit around one leg," Othick said, laughing. "He gets to the pool and jumps in naked. He swims 15 laps and then lays there naked. He was a character."

SOAP SUDS

Olson has long been known to never utter a curse word while coaching for three decades.

"He did have his sayings, though," said Muehlebach. "Like 'heck bent for election' instead of 'hell bent for leather.' He wouldn't even say hell."

In one practice, Mark Georgeson had had a difficult time attempting to score on Anthony Cook. And on one occasion when Cook rejected a Georgeson shot near the basket, Georgeson yelled an expletive loudly. What was worse, Olson was only two or three feet away just under the basket.

"Lute went through his whole routine," Muehlebach recalled. "He got into his face and told him that if he wanted to go back into the locker room to have his mouth washed out with soap that could be arranged."

On the next play, Cook rejected Georgeson again. This time Georgeson fell down and was just a couple of feet from Olson, who was still under the basket. Of course, Georgeson didn't curse, but ...

"This time, Mark yelled Judas Priest," said Muehlebach, "That was one of Lute's sayings. It was so dead quiet for about two minutes. We didn't know whether to laugh or not say anything. Lute just let it go. We moved on, but we were dying inside."

STROLLING WITH THE BULLS

It was advertised as running with bulls in Spain, but it was hardly that for the Wildcats. During Arizona's summer European tour where it played nine games against various teams one of the most anticipated activities was getting a chance to see bull fighting in Madrid, Spain.

It wasn't even close. No bull.

"They claimed we were going to a bull fight, but the ring was as big as someone's backyard," said Muehlebach. "Then the next thing you know they bring out some donkeys so people started to ride them. Then they bring out the bulls, and they were so old. Here we were thinking we were going to a bull ring with matadors in front of thousands of people. It was to be the greatest thing."

It wasn't. At least the players weren't impressed.

"One of Lute's friends was out there running around with the bulls," said Muehlebach. "That's how scary it was. It was totally harmless. It was more like strolling with the bulls."

Hot Ticket

By the time Arizona had gone to its first Final Four in 1988, everybody wanted in. The problem was those who hadn't heeded Olson's advice in 1984 to "Get your tickets now" were all but shut out by the late 1980s when it came to seeing the Cats live and in person.

Olson & Co. became a sold-out show beginning in 1988. And soon after, with many trying to get a glimpse of the Cats, tickets were becoming hot items in divorce and bankruptcy court.

"We'd usually hear of the divorces before they'd happen, because of the tickets and who they were going to be transferred to," said Judi Kessler, in charge of such matters back then.

What really became bizarre—and almost fanatical—was in the early 1990s when ticket holders needed to liquidate assets. One of the ways to make money was through game tickets and the rights that went with them. They became part of the bankruptcy process.

Back in 1990, the late Judge Lawrence Ollason decided to auction off tickets to help pay debtors' creditors. Newspaper ads were made. For fans who didn't have tickets at the time it seemed like the quickest way to get tickets—outside of a ticket holder dying so a seat would become available.

It proved to be profitable. Tickets went anywhere from $10,000 to $17,000.

And those bids were just for the rights to buy the tickets. The tickets themselves cost as little as $275 for the season back then, plus a premium for being part of the school's Wildcat Club.

In the first few bankruptcy auctions, six tickets brought in more than $50,000.

Fans and observers were astounded at the prices and lengths people would go to see the Cats. And at the time Kessler said there was no other school going through UA's problems, in part because it was the newfound love for the Cats, just a year or two removed from getting their first Final Four.

In the end, about 60-70 pairs of tickets had been auctioned off.

One winner was Robert and Carole Little, who picked up tickets after shelling out $13,300 for the pair.

"No matter the price, I was going home with tickets," Carole told the *Arizona Republic*. "I heard they were going for $20,000. To me, it was worth it. Anyone has a price for what they want."

UA never really liked what was going on with the tickets, although it was never out any money, because whoever took over the rights had to pay the premiums.

"The issue we had was that there was no transfer policy," said Kessler. "We used to allow transfers before 1988. If you had multiple seats you could transfer all but two seats. After the auctions, we started that 'no transfer policy' and tried to stop the courts from auctioning off the seats."

Eventually, Arizona won. Now, transfers happen only in the case of death of a spouse, divorce or if a person transfers them over to a business. No more third-party transfers are allowed.

SOAPY SITUATION

Flashy guard Orlando Vega didn't stay long at Arizona. He seemed like a fish out of water.

No one questioned his talent, but he was more of a scorer than a complete player.

"He wasn't afraid to shoot it," said Othick. "The first time he went into McKale and we scrimmaged, you could see he had talent. He came in, threw it off the backboard and dunked it. We all looked at one another and said, 'Who in the world is this guy?'"

But after four months in the program he was gone.

"He just didn't fit in," Othick said. "He had incredible talent, but he wasn't a team guy."

And he was a bit different. One day, in the fall semester, when Fraser, then a graduate assistant coach, was at his apartment, Vega came by asking for help with his dishwasher. The two lived in the same complex.

"His kitchen was flooded with soap," Fraser said. "Soap was all over the kitchen counter. It was like the scene from *The Brady Bunch*."

Fraser looked at Vega, a freshman, and asked, "What the hell did you do?"

He said all he did was push the start button and all the soap started to come out.

What he didn't tell him was that he didn't use dishwashing soap.

"He put Tide in the dishwasher. Incredible," Fraser said.

Chapter 7

STEVE KERR AND SEAN ELLIOTT

WHO IS STEVE KERR?

He has this image of an All-American type. A do-gooder. And he's all that and more. Kerr, a six-foot-three guard from California, was the poster boy of success for the UA program in the early 1980s. He was an up-and-comer who had to be reckoned with at all times.

"He epitomized the program; he epitomized Lute," said friend and former UA teammate Muehlebach. "He was this underdog who had a great work ethic. He suffered through a lot of personal tragedy, and a lot of people embraced him. They rallied around him."

It didn't hurt that Kerr never was flamboyant or egotistical and was great with the media.

Big Burden

Throughout the history of Arizona basketball, there have been a number of talented and accomplished players who have come through the program. But no player has been better than Sean Elliott. He holds the school record for points in a career at 2,555 and was UA's first consensus All-American. He was also the first and only player to lead the school in scoring every one of his four years. If Kerr is a favorite son, Elliott is Tucson's All-American, inasmuch as he grew up in Tucson.

Does he like the fact he has the label of being called the best player to ever put on an Arizona uniform?

"I don't mind it," he said. "It's a great honor. There are a lot of players out there and a lot of them set the table for me. And I had a lot of great teammates, so it's a great honor."

Plenty of teammates don't argue Elliott is the guy who established Arizona as, first, an up-and-coming team in the mid-1980s and then a team that arrived later in the decade when UA made deep runs into the NCAA tournament.

"Sean reminds me a lot of Tim Duncan," Kerr said. "The two stand out to me because they are great people. They have a rare combination of unbelievable talent and humility. Most people who are that skilled tend to be flamboyant or self-possessed and a bit selfish. For Sean to be that humble and that good is unbelievable. To be college player of the year and be as accommodating and so soft spoken yet fun is just awesome."

Throughout his career at Arizona, there wasn't a day he didn't go without signing an autograph, many times having to sign hundreds on game days. On typical game days, he'd have to sign anywhere from 100 to 200. And not that he had to, but he did it because he wanted to.

"He was always approachable," said former UA assistant Jessie Evans. "He was a guy who was always cracking jokes and mimicking others. He and A.C. Cook were always together and cutting up all the time. He was the No. 1 player in the country and as approachable as anyone."

He was constantly at functions, promoting the school as its poster boy for success.

It was often said that Elliott was the guy who could never say "No."

"That carried over until my first eight to 10 years in the NBA," Elliott said. "I was always doing stuff. I was asked to do things all the time."

On one occasion during his senior year, Olson asked Elliott to accompany him to a luncheon where the two would speak.

Upon driving back—about an hour before practice—Elliott was starving, having missed lunch between classes. Olson stopped to get something real quick.

"I saw him dip into his wallet like he was going to give me a $20 bill, and back then $20 was a lot of money for a college kid," Elliott said. "I was thinking, 'Great,' because I already had it spent in my head. I was going to get a couple of cheeseburgers, a Coke and keep the rest."

Elliott thought he had it made, and food for at least a day.

"But coach gave the $20 and told me to bring him back the receipt and the change," he said. "I'm thinking, 'this cheap old guy.' He didn't give me anything. And I'm the guy who decided to come back for his senior year. Couldn't he even give me $20? He didn't give me anything. He's as clean as they come."

HE'S A CAT

In late August 1983, Steve Kerr joined the Arizona family, beginning classes at UA.

Upon getting Kerr's commitment, Lute Olson said, "We feel fortunate to pick up a player of Steve's ability this late in the recruiting season. Steve is an excellent team player. Our staff is very impressed with the type of person Steve is."

Those were prophetic words from Olson, speaking of his one-time star. Everything held true in Kerr's five-year stay with UA.

Olson liked what he saw in Kerr from the start, seeing him in a number of summer league games late in July of 1983. Arizona had one more scholarship to give. But it took a while for Olson to get around to giving Kerr the scholarship.

Kerr called UA a number of times but didn't get a response from the coaches.

Finally, in mid-August, Kerr made a decision to verbally commit to the only school that offered him a scholarship—Cal State Fullerton.

"Arizona and Cal-State Fullerton both showed interest," Kerr said. "But Fullerton offered me a scholarship, and Arizona had not. I was hoping Arizona would, but I had not heard from Lute. I just figured they had lost interest, so I finally told Cal-State that I would come."

It came with hesitation, however. Deep down, Kerr, who had starred at Pacific Palisades High in California, wanted to go where he felt most comfortable—Arizona.

So Kerr's father, Malcolm, intervened, calling Olson to tell him Steve wanted dearly to go to Arizona but was a bit perplexed he hadn't heard back from UA's coaches.

"He called Lute and said that indeed they were offering a scholarship, but that also shows you they weren't exactly beating down my door," Kerr said. "But they did offer me the scholarship, and I jumped at the chance to come here."

It didn't come without some concern.

"I felt bad because I'd be reneging on the commitment," said Kerr, who did not sign a letter of intent with CSF. "But it was obvious I made the right decision, but it was one of the hardest things I had to do."

But Kerr, a 15-year NBA veteran and a member of five NBA title teams, said he never questioned his decision.

"I definitely wouldn't be where I am," he said. "I wouldn't have made the NBA, never would have had all the success."

FRENCH FRIED

About every four years, Arizona's Olson tries to take advantage of the rule allowing schools to take foreign summer tours, which eventually help with team chemistry and after, additional play for some who didn't play much the year before and preparation for the next season.

It's also a diversion for the players, who can gain culture from other countries. UA players took advantage of their trip to Europe to meet ... girls. As it turned out, it was the shy Kerr who played matchmaker or at least interpreter.

"I had taken French for a couple of years so I was translating for them," Kerr said, of his teammates. "I'd go to the post office with them and help them send postcards. I'd introduce girls to the guys. It was fun. I still regret taking French in school, because you never really have a chance to use it, but I had a chance there, so it was fun."

OPIE

As Kerr's popularity grew, a few columnists saw the resemblance between Kerr and fictional character Opie Taylor of Mayberry R.F.D, the television show. So in describing Kerr, a boy-next-door type with All-American qualities, writers found it easy to compare Kerr to the character.

Kerr had no problem with the comparison.

"It wasn't something people actually called me," he said. "My teammates didn't. I didn't care."

After all, it was a term of endearment.

TRAGEDY STRIKES

It's a morning few who followed Arizona basketball in the mid-1980s will ever forget. Kerr will never forget. At about 3 a.m. on January 18, 1984, Kerr got a call from Beirut, Lebanon, saying his father, Malcolm, had been assassinated by Arab gunmen. Mr. Kerr had been the American University president at the time.

Shocked, dismayed and hurt, Kerr was all those that early morning.

Olson said he wished someone had called the coaches first before talking to Steve about it, but "the pastor was concerned Steve would see it in the news first. It would have been much better for us to go up there and be with him. You can imagine being a kid and getting that call."

But as Kerr said, "Either way, somebody was going to have to tell me."

Soon after, he got a call from assistant coach Scott Thompson, who just had received a call from UA supporter George Kalil who was up early and heard the news on the radio.

"They took me to Carrows to eat at 5 a.m.," Kerr said. "We just sat and talked. It was awesome that they were there for support."

Later in the day, Kerr spent most it in Olson's office, sleeping and resting before practice was to start. Calls from national morning shows like *Good Morning America* and *The Today Show* called to ask if Steve could be on their shows. He declined.

There was a strange feeling throughout the day. His teammates did what they could to console him. That night, instead of staying in his place, he spent the night at Olson's house, where mother-figure Bobbi Olson comforted him.

"We called my mom from the house. I couldn't call from my dorm, because it wouldn't allow it," Kerr said. "Later on, I got in the hot tub with Steve, the Olsons' son. Bobbi later brought me a beer. It was great just having their support."

Kerr decided he was not going to travel to Beirut. It would have meant missing too much class time and the family would be back in the United States soon for two more memorials.

Moment of Kerr

Just two days after Kerr received word his father was assassinated, Kerr, then a freshman, decided to play in UA's game against Arizona State.

Before the game there was a moment of silence. Kerr came out with a towel draped over his head.

"It was strange," said Kerr. "Lute asked if we wanted to be out there and I said, 'Yes.' It was tough. What else can you say?"

Arizona proceeded to play rival ASU, a team UA hadn't beaten in nine straight games.

But that night—in a game dedicated to Kerr—he was the star. Kerr hit his first shot—a 25-footer—after entering the game with 12:58 left in the first half.

He finished with 12 points in 25 minutes of playing time. He left to a standing ovation in a 71-49 romp.

"It wasn't difficult to play; playing in the game seemed very natural," Kerr said. "It was a nice outlet for me to play. If I hadn't played I would have dwelled on it even more. I played well and we won. It was a crazy atmosphere. I remember going through 1,000 different emotions."

He did admit after the game, however: "It might have looked like I wasn't thinking of my dad, but I thought of him the whole time."

STEEEVE KEERRRRR

It didn't matter if it was a five-footer or a 25-footer, but every time Kerr hit a shot, the band, the crowd, anyone would respond with the elongated name of Steve Kerr.

Steeeve Keerrrrr!

"It was cool," Kerr said. "I don't know why the band started to repeat it."

It all started the first game back after his father was assassinated. Kerr chose to play. Play he did.

He hit his first shot, then his second and then his third.

"Three straight times he was the guy who scored," said then UA announcer Roger Sedlmayr, who called UA games for 18 seasons. "It seemed all I was saying was Steve Kerr, but after a while I elongated it. A game or two later the band caught on. They just started doing it. A year later it was not only the band doing it but everyone else."

Said friend Matt Muehlebach: "I can't think of a more unique way to show your applause to a player in any sport. It's just unique. I remember there were some Duke fans here at McKale Center for a game and they were saying, "Steeeve Keerrr" whenever he missed a shot."

To this day, whenever Kerr plays in exhibition games or the like, he still gets the elongated reply.

"I'm not surprised it's lasted," said Sedlmayr. "People ask me to do it all the time. It's a bit awkward doing it in public."

Then the Unthinkable

Oddly, four years later, Kerr would be on the receiving end of something unjust and undignified. Some UA fans don't attend UA vs. ASU games in Tempe because of it. That night, before Arizona was to face the Sun Devils, a group of ASU students started to taunt Kerr with "Go back to Beirut," "PLO, PLO," and "Where's your father?"

It was unthinkable how the ASU students taunted Kerr, whose father was assassinated four years earlier.

After the game, Kerr said, "Those people are the scum of the earth."

At the time, Kerr's teammates wanted to go into the stands and get the hecklers. They didn't. In the meantime, Kerr stewed.

"It was alcohol talking, just a few college kids that got out of hand," Kerr said. "It was crazy. I couldn't believe it. I went over to the bench and started to cry. I was rattled."

But not rattled enough to help the Sun Devils. He finished with 22 points. He also had five assists and no turnovers, a typical game for him.

"That was one of the few games where I remember playing angry," Kerr said. "I was old enough and experienced enough to channel my anger into my play."

Oddly, it's also a game where one of the only things he remembers from that game was former major league baseball player Wally Joyner of the California Angels coming over to say hello.

"He didn't know what was going on, but all he wanted to do was come over and say hi," Kerr said. "It's weird how I associate that with that game, but I remember it."

BRACE PROBLEMS

Elliott went to Arizona with a left knee problem, having injured his anterior cruciate ligament in high school. Yet, he still wore a brace on the knee for security.

But in his sophomore year, UA officials had enough of the brace Elliott was wearing.

"He wore that blue, plastic brace all the time," said Steve Condon, then the team's trainer. "It started to break down, the cover of the hinges started to come off."

UA started to look into getting another new one, one much better than the old one he had had for years. After playing San Diego State his sophomore year—two games into the season—UA decided to change the brace. Condon and others rented a car and drove up the coast to Carlsbad, California, to visit a brace company. That's where UA had him form-fitted for a new brace, although it took a while for them to get it.

"Instead of having wear to that old brace I taped his knee for a couple of games," Condon said. "His mother was very upset with me. She thought I was having him get rid of the brace. She thought I made the decision on my own, but then I told her we were getting a new brace, and she was fine with it."

Not at first.

"I played that San Diego State game without the brace and my mom was at the plane when it landed," Elliott said, laughing.

Through the years, he went through a number of braces, never really having a problem with the knee again.

Tucson's favorite son and consensus All-American Sean Elliott, celebrates another Arizona victory.

Home-Grown Kid

Sean Elliott was about 16 years old when Arizona coach Lute Olson was hired to replace the fired Ben Lindsey in 1983. That summer, Elliott, a skinny but talented basketball player, showed up at Olson's summer basketball camp.

"Here was this young, baby-faced product who came to our basketball camp," said Scott Thompson. "He was young and frail. We looked at him as a staff and said, "Maybe he'll blossom into a player we'll have to watch. His body had not matured. He didn't have the jumping ability he has now, and he was wearing a brace."

By committing and playing at Arizona, it was like a match made in heaven. Elliott didn't have to leave home to become a star, something he thought was a possibility before Olson arrived.

Before Elliott even played for UA he established himself with the then-current UA players, having played in pick-up games at the Tucson Racquet Club.

"One day Sean was guarded by Keith Jackson, and Sean shaked and baked him and dunked over him," said John Edger. "He closed down the gym with that one. Then Sean came in and didn't pass the ball much, but he was a good player."

Eventually, after Elliott committed and signed with UA, some of the players would go watch him play for Cholla High where he became a McDonald's All-American.

"We used to watch Sean play and we'd tease him that he was playing against a bunch of little kids, playing and beating a bunch of little Indians," Edger said.

Said Elliott: "They'd say stuff like that all the time, giving me plenty of grief."

But he gained their respect by showing up and playing with them in the pick-up games.

"When I committed I wanted to see how I stacked up against them," Elliott said. "I wanted to be with them, so I'd sneak in and play with them in pick-up games."

As for his future teammates showing up and seeing him play, "That was new to me. I guess they just liked watching basketball. Here I had college guys coming to see me play."

A HELLISH PRACTICE

The first day of practice for Elliott was the worst. In fact, he didn't know what he was getting into until he went through it.

"I was surprised no cops were there to give me a breathalyzer because I looked like I was drunk," Elliott said.

He was hardly drunk. He was fatigued, walking out of practice like something had hit him so hard he felt like dying. It was Olson, making his mark on the team and his star player.

"I thought I knew what to expect, but I didn't," Elliott said. "The level of intensity from high school to college was night and day. When I was running the first wind sprint, for some reason I couldn't make it, even though I had made them before."

It was nerves and anxiety, he thought.

"For some reason I just lost my stamina," he said. "If you didn't make the first sprint in a certain time you had to run it again, and that just compounded my problem. Then there was this defensive drill where you're placed in the middle, and the only way you can get out is if you get a deflection, and I just couldn't do it. Eventually I had to puke because I was so tired."

BAD MOVE

Early in Elliott's career in a game against Nevada Las Vegas, Arizona lost to the Rebels 92-87 in a tough, last-second game.

Despite Elliott being one of the team's best players, Olson ripped into him in a postgame tirade, after Elliott broke away from the designed play, hoping he'd win the game on his own. He didn't.

"Coach essentially called out his manhood, saying, 'You think you are better than these guys?' It was incredible," Bruce Fraser said. "I felt bad for Sean, but the time it was an awakening for him. As good as he was, he wasn't going to be a one-man team. We didn't feel that way, because we knew he wasn't that type of guy. No one on the team was mad at him. He WAS the best guy."

Elliott, however, knew he had done wrong.

"It was my fault," Elliott said. "I thought I could make a play, and I didn't. He let me have it. He tore me not one but two new ones. He didn't let me off the hook for that one."

A year later—as is typical with many players in the program, it's said—Elliott admitted he wanted to transfer. Kerr was out with a knee injury, and the team had no clear-cut leader.

"It was the hardest year I had," he said. "I cried to my mom every week on the phone. It was one of those years where you just had to grow up. Coach rides you extra hard. And we had lost Steve. We struggled to make the tournament. We had a lot of tough practices, and I got my share of practices where I got yelled at."

JUST A NORMAL GUY

By Elliott's junior year, most everyone wanted a piece of him. Autograph hounds searched him out, news agencies held to every word and sound bite.

Then there were the days when magazines and big-time newspapers wanted to spend the day with him.

One time, a reporter from *USA TODAY* spent a day in Tucson following Elliott around campus and to class. It was very unusual in that the reporter was older and seemingly out of place, following Tucson's sweetheart and college basketball's best player.

"It was hysterical," Elliott said. "Everyone was wondering what was going on. And it seemed kind of weird. All my teammates were like, 'Who is this guy?' In class there were cameras and the professors were like, 'Who was my new side-kick?'"

And all this time, all he wanted was the label of being "a normal guy."

That's what he was—a hometown guy who stayed close to home only to become a hometown hero in the town's must-see sport.

"I didn't like being singled out in the newspaper," he said. "I didn't like to pick up the papers and just seeing what I had done in the papers. I didn't feel it was good for our team. I just thought the others should be recognized, too. But the stories were about me and what I did, leaving the other guys out. That was uncomfortable. The other guys worked very hard, and everyone should be recognized. They should have been recognized."

BOYS GONE WILD

It was a nice, beautiful spring day when Arizona seniors Anthony Cook and Elliott decided to go out and test drive a new car. It was also on a day when the seniors were supposed to be at a dinner later in the day. But they got a little side-tracked—they got in a car accident, and not just a small one.

"We got in the car and drove it around," Elliott said. "I was driving at first, but then A.C, said, 'Wow, this car is fast and powerful.'"

The two changed seats, and no sooner had they left for another ride they were upside down.

"We were both in it, he took a turn fast that required a lot of care," Elliott said. "It wasn't like we flipped like the Dukes of Hazzard where we were flying high through the air. We got on an embankment and it turned on its side and all of a sudden it flipped slowly and we slid down."

Both were fine but didn't make the dinner.

"It was pretty scary," Fraser said. "They were both freaked out."

Chapter 8

EARLY 1990S

SHAQ ATTACKED

Arizona played host to Louisiana State and Shaquille O'Neal in 1991. It was a huge media spectacle, and there was a buzz in the air. It turned out to be an easy win for Arizona, but O'Neal had the last jab against Rooks, who outplayed him for a day.

"Shaq said, 'I don't care how good you play, I'm still the No. 1 draft pick,'" Rooks said. "I wanted to come back (and say something) but I just thought, 'You're right.'"

At the time, Rooks said, "It was the greatest line I had ever heard." And that coming from a guy who had all the one-liners.

Years later they turned out to be teammates for the Los Angeles Lakers.

"And every year for three years at least three or four different times a month he'd talk some shit about that," Rooks said. "Until this day, he still talks about that."

Size didn't matter when it came to Damon Stoudamire, one of UA's toughest competitors in the backcourt.

EN GARDE

The college basketball world didn't know it to begin the season, but it quickly learned Arizona would eventually have the best backcourt in the country during the 1993-94 season. The reason? Senior Khalid Reeves and junior Damon Stoudamire.

Together, they became the school's best backcourt one-two punch in history. Reeves averaged 24.2 points a game; Stoudamire averaged 18.3 points per game. They combined for 45 percent of Arizona's points.

"They had to do a lot for us to be successful that year," Olson said.

"You look at backcourt combinations we've had—Mike Bibby, Miles Simon and Jason Terry—and we've had some good ones. But as a pair those two (Stoudamire, Reeves) had to play all the time. And what Khalid did in the playoffs, averaging 27 points, was remarkable. The two did exactly what they had to do for us."

And they were the best of friends.

"It's not surprising that the great players gravitate to one another," said then-assistant Jessie Evans. "They enjoyed each other's company. And they were so different. Damon was such a neat freak, so much so, that eventually no one would want to live with Damon."

SKINNER SUITS UP

Arizona needed help with bodies early in the 1991-92 season. There were injuries and academic problems. So Charlie Skinner, a team manager who had some basketball skills, suited up.

"Unbeknownst to me, Chris Mills went to Coach Olson to ask him if I could help by suiting up," Skinner said.

Olson said it could be done. Skinner traveled almost half the season as a player and not as a manager. Arizona almost got to the point where it needed Skinner's services.

"We were playing East Tennessee State in the NCAA tournament and there were four guys with four fouls so there was a chance that I was going to play," Skinner said. "It was awesome. I almost got a chance to play. But it was great playing against guys like Khalid Reeves and Damon Stoudamire."

His playing days were short-lived. In early 1993, Skinner was back to being a manager.

"Lute even liked him more than he liked me," Othick said.

But one day, Skinner fell out of favor after missing the team bus and flight on a trip back to Tucson after a game in New Orleans.

After UA beat New Orleans 72-69, Skinner went out with a couple of players but decided to stay out later than the others.

After all, he was in New Orleans and girls were around.

"We were in a bar, I drank and passed out," Skinner said. "I woke up and looked at my watch and it seemed like I had time."

Problem was he never changed his watch when the team arrived in New Orleans. It was still on Tucson time where it was an hour behind.

"It seemed like it was kind of light outside," he said. "I just missed the bus and the plane."

Problems didn't end there. When he attempted to use his ATM card the machine took it, leaving him with no money.

"Then there was a Mary Kay convention so I got bumped from 13 flights to Dallas (a connection to Tucson). It was the worst," he said.

Not exactly.

Upon arriving—finally—to Tucson, Olson demoted him from senior manager.

"I learned a lot of good lessons out of it," he said. "You're there for work and not to have too much fun. But working for Coach Olson was the best."

WATER PROBLEMS

Khalid Reeves was notorious for being afraid of the water. No matter the situation.

But early in his career, Othick was able to convince Reeves to get into the water—in his Jacuzzi.

"I had a party one time at my place and he was afraid to get in," Othick said. "He was standing in it and was still scared."

All it took was some convincing from some girls and Reeves was in for good.

"He wasn't going to get in, but there were four or five good-looking girls in there so he decided to do it," Othick said. "He got in and said, 'This isn't bad.'"

HELP! HELP!

One of the funnier moments in UA's time together while playing summer exhibition games the summer of 1993 was when the team went out on a boat after a few days in Australia.

This just a day after they were attempting to teach Reeves how to swim.

The day before, Reeves & Co. went snorkeling—it was his first time—and as the guys went out just a few feet from shore where Reeves could put his feet in the water and look down

Khalid Reeves had one of UA's best senior seasons ever, becoming the only player in school history to score more then 800 points in a season.

as he snorkeled, Reeves jumped up and said, "Hey, they're fish down there!"

Well, of course there are. His teammates had a big laugh.

The next day, they took a boat to the Great Barrier Reef and convinced Reeves he could swim, but that it was safe because the boat would not be too far off from where they were.

He decided to do it, but after a few moments saw that the boat was about 30 to 40 feet away.

"He just panicked," said McLean. "He became dead weight. It was a struggle. He was so strong, but we were able to get him back in the boat."

All can laugh about it now, including Reeves.

"I'm not a good swimmer," he said. "I was raised in the city. I should have never gotten into the water in the first place. But they convinced me and I was out of my element. I still don't now how to swim."

Devastating Loss

In 1993, a season after reaching the Sweet 16, Arizona appeared headed for another deep run into the NCAA Tournament. Arizona was ranked as high as No. 2 twice in the season, including the season's final week before it lost in the final two games of the regular season.

But those losses were nothing compared to what happened a week later in the first round of the NCAA Tournament when Arizona was shipped to Atlanta to play 14th-seed East Tennessee State in the Southeast region.

Arizona was a No. 3 seed.

Arizona was outquicked, outhustled and outeverythinged in a major upset that saw ETSU beat UA 87-80. ETSU used its smaller lineup to hit threes and run the court with ease over the taller Arizona Wildcats.

"That game will haunt me for life," said Othick, a senior back then. "I still don't know how we lost it. I didn't score. It was the only one I didn't score in my entire senior year."

It's such a bad memory for Othick he has refused to see a replay.

"You know that numb feeling you get sometimes, well, that's the feeling I had during the game and how I felt afterward," Othick said. "I think because we went with a big lineup that hurt. And they had one of those nights where they hit all their three-pointers. And we had these 6-11 guys trying to chase around these 6-5 guys."

HE'S A WINNER

Throughout the years at Arizona there have been a number of All-Americans and future pro standouts, but there has been no one more successful than former guard Matt Muehlebach, who played from 1987 to 1991.

In that time, Arizona went 109-29, making him the winningest player in school history.

"I was smart enough to pick the right school," said Muehlebach, jokingly, now a lawyer in Tucson. "I had a good idea who would be good for a number of years."

Actually, he was a big part of Arizona's success. He was a three-year starter and eventually the team's captain in 1991-92.

He was destined to be a Wildcat, having grown up in Northern California watching Arizona a number of times as it swung through to play Stanford and California in the Pacific 10 Conference.

"I remember seeing Steve Kerr and Brock Brunkhorst play (in the mid-1980s)," Muehlebach said. "I'd wonder who were these blond, blue-eyed guys playing. Back then, they were just a fun team to watch because they were getting better. And if you were a basketball fan, you knew who Lute Olson was and you knew his reputation."

TRIPLE THREAT

When Muehlebach registered the school's first triple-double it came from perhaps the most nondescript player in the era of formidable stars. Sean Elliott didn't get one. Neither did Steve Kerr or Tom Tolbert or Anthony Cook.

But on March 9, 1990, Muehlebach had 10 points, 11 rebounds and 10 assists in an 80-57 win against Southern California.

"Lute always went into halftime going over the rebound stats, and I remember him telling us I had six or seven, and at that point it was my career high," Muehlebach said. "I remember thinking I had a bunch of assists. But I didn't think a whole lot about it."

Yet, while he was having success with rebounds and assists, he struggled offensively.

"Lute knew I was a point away from it, and he called a couple of plays for me and he never did that," Muehlebach said. "On both plays I got fouled and then I missed the first of a one and one. All I needed was one point. I guess it was the pressure."

He eventually picked up the point late in the game.

"Let's just put it this way," Muehlebach said, "it wasn't the most dazzling of triple-doubles."

UA has had eight more triple-doubles since.

WALK ON, BYE BYE

In the summer of 1991 freshman Brian Nelson enjoyed his visit to Arizona and Tucson so much he decided to join the team as a walk-on. He was the first walk-on in the Lute Olson era at Arizona.

What was surprising was how much publicity Nelson received, particularly at the annual Pac-10 Conference media event when, despite Arizona being one of the nation's top teams, the media wanted to talk more about Nelson, someone who would have played little had he played at all.

It caught Olson by surprise in that Nelson was just a walk-on, and the key players were seniors Matt Othick and Sean Rooks.

But two weeks after the media event, Nelson decided UA wasn't the place for him and he quit the team.

Fame was fleeting.

JUST A SUGGESTION

It seemingly happens every other year. Arizona schedules a tough, nonconference opponent somewhere in the East and then arrives late into the evening the night before the game. And—unfortunately for UA—the game is typically a noon to mid-afternoon game where the team doesn't have enough time to get acclimated to the situation or get enough sleep to be prepared for what's ahead.

It happened in 2000 when UA faced Illinois in the Great Eight in Chicago after Arizona had to deal with airline delays; it happened against Louisiana State (more airline delays); and in other nonconference games.

One game especially was biting for Muehlebach, a team captain in 1991-92.

Arizona arrived late the night before having to play tough Pittsburgh. UA didn't arrive until midnight, and the players didn't get to their rooms until 1 a.m. for a noon game.

Then came as Muehlebach said, "One of my greatest captain's moves ever."

He suggested to an assistant coach that perhaps it was best that the team get a chance to sleep in longer than usual so the team could be rested for the big game, all the while passing on the scheduled brisk walk Olson planned for the team early in the morning.

"It was with the consideration that we'll all get charged up for the game," said Muehlebach, now able to laugh about it. "Well, that went over like a turd in a punch bowl."

By the early morning at the team breakfast, Olson made an announcement that, "He was going on a brisk walk and anyone who cared about the game that day can go, too," Muehlebach recalled.

"Eventually, I just don't think it mattered—brisk walk or not—because we got our asses kicked," Muehlebach said, of the 100-92 loss.

POOL PARTY

Over the last few years Olson has had more and more get-togethers at his home with his former players. One party—said to be a reunion of players—had an unusual experience when Steve Kerr, Matt Muehlebach, Tom Tolbert and Jud Buechler all looked at one another and then dared each other to jump into the pool—clothed.

"It was kind of the first time we became friends with Lute more so than he was our coach," said former UA player/grad assistant coach Bruce Fraser. "When we were players he was tough to get to know, keeping himself at a distance at a professional level."

"The guys were having a good time when Fraser said Kerr went to Muehlebach and said, 'How much to go in the pool? Right here, right now. Will you go in?' Matt called Steve out. Then they asked me. I said if Steve goes in, I'll go in. Tolbert then said the same. Then we all agreed to do it. We all jumped in."

Later in the night, everyone got involved—including Olson.

"It was one of those things where you think or wonder if Coach is going to kick you out of his house and hate you forever or love it," Fraser said. "He loved it. He got in the jacuzzi with us with his clothes on. Bobbi was bringing us beverages. It was awesome. We ended up telling stories until 2 a.m. in that jacuzzi."

Olson debated Fraser's version saying, he wasn't about to go in the water with his clothes on, so he changed into his swimsuit and got in.

"I knew if I didn't get that swimsuit on I'd be going in with my clothes on," Olson said, figuring he'd be pushed in or something.

Added Othick, "See that's why Coach Olson is so smart. He was always thinking ahead."

To Redshirt, or Not to Redshirt

At the beginning of the 1992-93 season, Joe McLean seemed destined to be a prime candidate to redshirt. He was a freshman playing behind Ray Owes, Reggie Geary, Chris Mills. It seemed logical.

Then came the game against Rhode Island in early January where Arizona NEEDED McLean, if only for his hustle and grit.

In a matter of minutes, McLean, sporting kneepads and a determination, sparked UA to a victory.

He was all over the floor, diving for balls, creating havoc.

By the end of the game, McLean had played 19 minutes, had 11 points, two steals, three assists and three rebounds.

"During the Christmas break we were practicing at Bear Down and Chris (Mills) wasn't playing all that well or at least not up to his ability. So here was this opportunity to get him going, too. They had mentioned that I might play, but (he didn't think it would happen)."

Then against Rhode Island, with Arizona struggling, Olson went down the bench and told McLean to get in. McLean promptly put the Cats ahead with consecutive baskets, making it 58-57 with 12 minutes left.

"Luckily I actually had a uniform on underneath my warmups," McLean said. "Sometimes if you're not playing, some guys don't even wear a uniform under there."

UA Is STREAKING

At the time, it was Arizona's all-time best win streak where no one seemed to even come close to the Cats. Indeed, 1992-93 seemed to be a magical-type year and one where many thought they could return to the Final Four after a five-year absence.

The streak started when UA beat Delaware State in the first game of the Fiesta Bowl Classic and eventually ended when UA fell to California 74-71 at the Oakland Coliseum. In total, Arizona reeled off 19 straight wins behind Chris Mills, Damon Stoudamire and Khalid Reeves.

"I still contend that one through 12, that team was one of the best teams I've played on," said McLean. "We had the players and no one could contend with us. We went 17-1, still one of the best records in the Pac-10. We were unstoppable … then came the first round of the NCAAs."

Arizona lost to Santa Clara 64-61 in the tournament's first round, finishing the season 24-4 overall.

War Breaks Out

On January 17, 1991, Arizona was to face Arizona State in its annual rivalry game. But that day—of all days—war had started in Kuwait. No one had basketball on their minds. Arizona eventually beat ASU, 74-71, in Tempe. But the mood was somber.

"Back then there wasn't a rivalry, because we never lost to them," said Muehlebach. "But it was a strange game, pretty sobering.

"And what was sobering about the time was that I always heard about my grandfather enlisting into the war and wanting to get in. I remember thinking I was of the age back then and it was pretty scary."

An Inspiration

To say walk-on Cliff Johns bucked the odds wouldn't be enough in telling his story.

Johns, a 6-2 guard, became Olson's second walk-on in the program but first to make it through the season. He was an inspiration to all but more specifically a role model to many because he was a Native American from Winslow, Arizona.

After transferring from Northern Arizona, Johns was spotted at the UA Recreation Center playing pick-up basketball. He transferred to UA because of its architecture program. Ironically, Johns had asked at least twice if he could walk on to the team. He was turned down twice. Upon getting the invite to tryout, Johns couldn't have been happier, pumping his fists and jumping up and down after putting down the phone.

Eventually Johns was placed on partial scholarship, although he was on a full architecture scholarship.

"It was great for the entire Navajo community," Olson said, of Johns's accomplishment. "He was widely known in the community."

Very well known. Johns spoke to a number of schools during his time at UA and continues to speak to children today.

"It did draw ripples in terms of Native American males. It helped them reach goals at that level," Johns said. "It did open doors. It gave them and me an opportunity to show that given a chance you can make it at that level."

THE STREAK ENDS

With a flick of a wrist from UCLA guard Darrick Martin at the buzzer, the Wildcats' 71-game winning streak came to a screeching halt. Arizona lost 89-87. Martin hit a running 15-footer over freshman guard Damon Stoudamire for the win. Just like that, Arizona's streak was over at 71, the 10th longest streak in NCAA history and 10 games short of the school record established at Bear Down Gym (1945-51).

"A lot of people ask if the pressure was building, but from a coaching standpoint it wasn't that big a deal," Olson said. "There were some great games in there that we won because they didn't want to be the guys who ended the streak."

People like Sean Elliott, Steve Kerr, Kenny Lofton and Anthony Cook helped build it. Then it fell to the dreaded Bruins.

"It was disappointing especially because it was UCLA. They were always so cocky. Nobody liked losing to UCLA," Sean Elliott said.

For Matt Othick, who was a senior then, the loss "was sickening" in part because he was replaced by Damon Stoudamire on the final play.

"I was upset because I always finished games," Othick said. "I think Coach Olson was concerned about Martin's penetration, but what he did was shoot right over Damon, something he couldn't have done to me. I had a long-running, head-to-head competition with Martin also. We were the top two guards on the west coast coming out of high school, so it stung even more to watch that shot from the bench. It was the only home game I lost in my career. But it was an amazing run that never seemed to end. As a player you felt like there was no way anyone could beat us at McKale. Between Coach O's preparation and our amazing fans, it was magical."

Olson said many of the victories came through the fans.

"It ended up being a real compliment to them and they took it that way, too," Olson said. "They were here to do everything they could to help us win."

Chapter 9

MID-1990s

First Practices

It was a much-ballyhooed class of five. UA's Fab Five. Reggie Geary, Joseph Blair, Corey Williams, Etdrick Bohannon and Joe McLean. There was a player for every position for the surging Wildcats. And they proved to be pretty good right away. In the first days of pick-up games, the youngsters showed they were to be noticed.

"One of my first thoughts arriving at Arizona was seeing seven-footer Ed Stokes and thinking he was the biggest human being I had ever seen," said Geary. "On top of that, he did a dunk so hard it seemed to have shook the whole gym and every freshman. It was just his way of reminding us that he WAS the biggest player we had ever seen."

It didn't, however, deter the freshmen from playing well in the early moments of the 1992-93 season.

"We proceeded to put a beating on the upperclassmen," said Geary, reminding the upperclassmen were Damon Stoudamire, Chris Mills, Khalid Reeves, among others. "We were so giddy, because it was our first taste of the college level together."

During one of the first pick-up games, an inadvertent elbow thrown by Ed Stokes broke the nose of Joseph Blair.

"Blood was everywhere, and Joseph's nose was broken," said Geary. "But being freshmen we were so excited about beating the upperclassmen that we encouraged and begged Joseph to continue. After all, we were beating the guys we had seen on TV and had admired. We didn't want that feeling to end. JB plugged his nose with tissue, and we continued to beat them the rest of the day. That was a big confidence boost for all of us freshmen."

Needless to say, Geary pointed out, it was the last time they beat the upperclassmen.

"They brought us down to earth every chance they had," Geary said. "But no matter what happened the rest of the season, they couldn't take that day away from us."

Olson Out, Rosborough In

For the first time in 39 years, Olson missed a game, having to lay on his back after injuring it earlier in the week after lifting weights. X-rays showed no damages but doctors did find a couple of abnormalities in his vertebrae that caused inflammation.

"It was strictly a muscular thing," Olson said. "I had been lifting weights and I pushed it the wrong way, and I didn't realize it until the next day when I had a hard time getting out of bed."

In place of Olson, assistant Jim Rosborough took over with the help of assistants Jessie Evans and Phil Johnson.

"I'll be honest, about an hour before the game," Rosborough said, "I did experience what appendicitis feels like."

Arizona won the game, beating LaSalle 92-76 at McKale Center. Olson called in his thoughts at halftime to help with things.

"As a coach and it's your team out there, you kind of feel like it's a hopeless situation," Olson said.

Said Damon Stoudamire: "I'm pretty sure he was at home, yelling at the TV at times."

There were some problems, however. Joseph Blair was going through some disciplinary problems.

"I asked Lute how he wanted to deal with it and he said, 'You deal with it,'" Rosborough said. "I don't recall starting Joseph. And the only other controversy was that Michael Dickerson wanted to play more. I might have gone in and tried to put him in late and he didn't want to go in."

THE SHRUG

It was a game Arizona had no business winning. Cincinnati, under coach Bob Huggins came in ranked fifth, and seemingly invincible against a Wildcat team that, by all appearances, was still searching for an identity that February of 1996.

But playing in its own backyard—Phoenix—in the 7-Up Shootout didn't hurt the Cats as an upset Huggins eventually pointed out. Most of the 11,112 fans at Veterans Memorial Coliseum were pulling for UA. And in the end they went home happy after UA won, 79-76.

"I remember watching ESPN afterward and them showing Huggins had destroyed their locker room (after the game)," recalled Miles Simon, the hero of the game. "He was pissed."

In part because the underdog Cats rallied from a nine-point deficit with six minutes left. Arizona was helped by Cincinnati's failure to inbound the ball with two seconds left with the scored tied at 76.

"That was a real good Cincinnati team," said Olson. "I knew we'd have to play as well as we could to pull off a win. When they had the ball and they took a timeout I just felt there were only two things that were going to happen: we'd lose or go into overtime."

But on the play, Cincinnati lost the ball and Arizona got a miracle when Simon hit a 65-foot bank shot at the buzzer for the upset. All Olson could do in the end was shrug his shoulders and go shake Huggins's hand.

"How can you ever count on something like that?," Olson said.

What it also did was give Olson his 500th career coaching victory.

"I'm not into counting games, but when you have a game like that, for your 500th win, you don't forget it," Olson said. "I would not remember it unless something like that happened—if it were not so special."

ESPY NOMINATED

From that game, Simon's 65-foot game saver was nominated for an ESPY, an annual award given by ESPN. It was up for play of the year. It didn't win.

"I should have won it," Simon said. "I really wanted to win it."

It wasn't like he didn't go unnoticed for it. It's still fondly remembered because it was so improbable.

"When I got home after the game I had 25 messages waiting for me," Simon said. "One was from my high school coach's son who back then used to work on trick shots after practice. He said, 'OK, you win with that one. That was the ultimate shot.'"

CLINTON WATCHING

The scene was a bit surreal. Arizona was back at the Final Four—this time in Charlotte, North Carolina, in 1994—and it was facing Arkansas with coach Nolan Richardson. None other than president Bill Clinton decided to attend the game. After all, he was the former governor of Arkansas, and he wanted to root on his Razorbacks.

Upon being asked his thoughts about Clinton coming to the game, Blair was asked if he was a Democrat or a Republican.

"Neither," Blair said, "I'm a basketball player."

The crowd and players were a bit perturbed that before the Final Four everyone had to go through metal detectors and tight security because of Clinton's attendance.

"I didn't give a flying (expletive) if he was at the game or not," said Blair. "First of all, he was just one fan. And he surely wasn't there to help me. He might as well stayed at the White House as far as I was concerned. He made it difficult—security and everything—for everyone to play the game, and it was our game. If anything, he may have taken away from the players who busted their ass to get there. He took some of the spotlight. We all worked hard to get there."

Arizona's Corey Williams couldn't agree with his teammate.

Williams, a political science major, welcomed the attendance of Clinton in Charlotte. Forget about all the security and forget that Clinton was rooting for Arkansas.

Joseph Blair, the outspoken one, was tough to handle near the basket.

"It was a nice distraction," Williams said. "Whenever the leader of the free world goes to a basketball game you're playing in that's something you can always talk about—forever."

THE YAPPER

It was often said Williams spoke just for the sake of speaking. Argued for the sake of arguing. His teammates shuddered when he was around and wanted to talk about politics, economics, well, anything.

"Corey is one of those guys who can be really frustrating to listen to," said his former roommate Damon Stoudamire. "He can say things that just blow your mind. And I don't know why he does it. He gets into one of those zones and just phases out."

Jokingly, Olson wondered if Williams talked in his sleep.

"If his waking hours are 17 hours, then 16 hours, 50 minutes of those are spent talking. He talks about everything. Who knows what he talks about," Olson said. "Reggie (Geary) is like that, too. It's an interesting conversation between the two, because neither of them is listening to the other."

Years later, Williams said he "didn't talk just to talk."

"I know the things I talk about," he said. "I know what I know, and I know the things I don't know, so I don't talk about things I don't know about. Reggie just talks. Us together was a bad combination, because Reggie always thought he was right, so he and I used to argue."

It could've been about anything. Most of the time it was.

"Everyone (teammates) would come up to me and say, 'You were right, and Reggie didn't have a clue,'" Williams said, laughing. "But I'm sure they told Reggie the same thing about me."

PLAY ON MONDAY!

After getting to the Final Four in 1994 with mostly juniors and sophomores, the mood at Arizona was upbeat to say the least for the next season. Going in, *Basketball Times* had UA at No. 1 with a large photo of team leader Damon Stoudamire on the cover.

Thus came the team theme: "Play on Monday," meaning that Arizona already had tasted the Final Four experience having played on Saturday for the semifinals so now the next step would be to play on Monday for the title. And Arizona had a good chance with the nucleus back.

"That was our goal," Blair said. "Then Ben, Damon couldn't play (because of NCAA violations) and I had sprained my ankle earlier the week. I did the jump ball, but I just couldn't go."

It turned out to be key because Miami of Ohio's Devin Davis proved to be too much for the Wildcats, both offensively and on the boards. Davis, a six-foot-seven jumping jack sporting a funky hairdo, had a game-high 24 points and 15 rebounds in the 71-62 defeat of Arizona.

"It was a frustrating game for me," said Blair, who played 14 minutes and scored just three points. "We were nothing without them (Davis, Stoudamire)."

1,000 REASONS FOR LOSS

UA was riding high during the NCAA Tournament in 1996 despite the absence of Blair. It had beaten Valparaiso 90-51 in the first round and had easily disposed of Iowa 87-73 in round No. 2. Then came the meeting with Kansas in Denver at the Sweet 16.

But the night before Arizona was to face Kansas, Joe McLean suffered from food poisoning, after eating a salad for dinner.

"I always had Thousand Island dressing, and they didn't have any," McLean said, of the restaurant. "I told them, 'You need to go find that dressing, make it happen'—and they did."

Why was the salad dressing suspected? McLean was the only UA player to have it.

McLean became sick that night, going to the hospital at 2 a.m. until 4 p.m., just a couple of hours before tip-off. Despite being ill, McLean started the game and drew the assignment of having to stop Kansas big man Raef LaFrentz. McLean was still too ill to contribute much.

Olson still feels had Arizona had a healthy McLean, UA would have won that game. Kansas won 83-80, after UA had held the lead with just under a minute left.

"Joe was one of our best defenders and a tough, hard-nosed competitor," said Olson. "He made everyone else compete that much harder."

Arizona had come this close to making its third trip to the Final Four.

"The way we looked at it was that if we beat Kansas," Simon said, "we were going to go to the Final Four. We didn't think Syracuse could beat us a second time (that season)."

It just wasn't meant to be.

THE LETTER

Dylan Rigdon was in his early teens when he received his first piece of recruiting mail from UA. It came from former UA assistant Kevin O'Neill.

"It was my first college letter I had ever received," said Rigdon. "It was from O'Neill, and the first name and my last name were spelled incorrectly. It was something like Alien Rugdon or something like that. It wasn't even close."

By the time it came to deciding where to go, Rigdon was no longer high on UA's list, so he enrolled at UC-Irvine, playing there two years before deciding to transfer to UA.

"Back then, it was cool to receive letters, but they also didn't mean much," Rigdon said. "At least you're on the radar, although they were probably sending thousands of letters. For me, it was a little boost of confidence."

Ridgon decided to transfer to Arizona only after Rooks played with Rigdon in a Los Angeles summer league, convincing him that UA needed a shooting guard because Casey Schmidt decided to transfer.

"I told Sean there was no way I thought I could play there, but then the more I played in the summer league, the more I thought I could," Rigdon said.

Then came the transfer, although Arizona coach Lute Olson had his doubts early that Rigdon could cut it.

"I would have said I doubt it," said Olson, of Rigdon's contributions, "because his defense was so bad at the time. The effort was so lacking. And his offense suffered because he didn't have the defense to get extended playing time to get the confidence he needs for his shot."

By the end of his career, Rigdon averaged 16 minutes a game and 7.0 points per game. He also hit a team-leading 41.1 percent of his three-point shots.

"All I wanted to do was come to Arizona," Rigdon said. "I just wanted to play for Lute Olson. At the time—and it still is—Arizona was one of the best programs in the West. I couldn't pass up that opportunity."

Team Dissension

Eleven games games into the 1995-96 season, and Arizona had already won the NIT preseason title, but players were beginning to show unhappiness.

Yet, Arizona was 10-1 going into its trip to the Bay Area to face California and Stanford.

Arizona proceeded to lose to California, 75-99, and again to Stanford, 71-80.

It was the first time Arizona had been swept in the Bay since the 1991-92 season.

It was then players revealed the unhappiness.

"We have problems that don't have anything to do with basketball," Corey Williams said at the time. "Until we get those problems settled, we're not going to win again."

Upon hearing some of the players being disgruntled, Olson said, "If these guys say that (that there are problems) they are closer to it than we are. If that's the case, they have to correct it individually."

Upon further review it was the veterans who were worried about playing time, as freshmen Miles Simon and Michael Dickerson were taking some of their minutes.

"I had lost my job to Michael Dickerson, and Joe McLean was coming off the bench in favor of Miles Simon," Williams said. "Then there was Reggie, the two kids, Joseph Blair and Ben Davis. Normally, that was a good lineup, because those two (Simon, Dickerson) earned their positions.

"But it was too much too soon. And sometimes that can cause problems for players."

McLean agreed, saying the seniors had to adjust to the two freshmen playing more as the season went along.

"It was a case where the team was chock full of seniors, and we all wanted to play individually well and as a team," McLean said. "We wanted playing time. But early in the season we hadn't found our roles. I wasn't happy. Corey wasn't happy, but it was nothing against Coach. After that we became a team of five captains (the seniors)."

An Eye-Opener

It isn't unusual to see former UA greats return to play against current UA players during the summer or school year. In the fall of 1994, Steve Kerr and Khalid Reeves returned to play against the Wildcats, giving them a chance to hang around campus, still being connected to the program.

"I like things like that," said Simon. "I remember when Steve came and played. It was funny because Steve was out there working on specific things, working on things to improve their game. They're not out there to bust the college player's ass."

At least not on that day. Simon said he remembered calling his father, Walt, after watching Steve.

"I said, 'Steve Kerr came to play, but he's not very good, Dad,'" Simon said, smiling. "The next day Steve came out and hit about 87 percent of his three-pointers. It was right in my face every time. He was just playing around the day before.

"As for Khalid, he could just turn it on and off whenever he wanted to. The thing about the pros is they can turn it on and off whenever they want to or when they need to."

Snow Job

Arizona was still searching for an identity in January of 1996. After beating Arizona State 108-76, it seemed Arizona was headed in that direction.

Then came its scheduled game against up-and-comer St. Joseph's.

The game never happened. Arizona officials claimed a major east coast snowstorm was going to keep the team home because they feared for UA's safety while traveling for a non-conference game.

St. Joe's coach, Phil Martelli, was furious. "Any talk of rescheduling the game (is moot) because I wouldn't play them if the NCAA seeded us to play them," he said. "If that's the big-time... you don't do that to CYO teams."

Martelli had been looking forward to face UA just days after taking then No. 1 Massachusetts into overtime at home.

"There is no question I am upset," Martelli said, at the time. "The game was not canceled. It was a unilateral decision by one of the big boys to not play a contracted game. No amount of disguise or pompousness is going to change my mind. UA decided not to play this game when they saw the UMass score, and they realized there was a chance they'd be in for a difficult game. Anything else is a smokescreen."

There were some theories. That weekend, unconfirmed rumors started to circulate that Blair was academically ineligible. He would not have been able to play.

But Jim Livengood, Arizona's athletic director, said it was his decision to call it off, citing weather reports, airline schedules and the players' safety.

"I had heard the Joseph (rumors) and this and that," Livengood said, "but in my heart of hearts, I have kids and I was really concerned about the weather. It was my call. I told the president (of the university, Manuel Pacheco) what I wanted to do and he said, 'If that's what you want to do, then that's what you do.'"

Livengood did, with the school eventually having to pay a reported $80,000 for the cancellation.

"Phil and I have talked about it and he's a good person," Livengood said, "and it not only hurt him, but it was a chance to beat a big-time team playing in Philly."

Years later, Livengood didn't second guess his decision.

"We felt very good about it," he said. "If I was on the outside looking in, I would have had some questions too, but I'm comfortable about what happened. It was the right thing to do.

"What if something would have happened?"

ACADEMIC PROBLEM

Days after UA cancelled its game with Saint Joseph's, news broke that Blair was academically ineligible. It was just days before the spring semester was to start. Blair was not allowed to play under an Arizona Board of Regents rule, one that states a player must have at least a 2.0 grade-point average in order to participate in intercollegiate athletics.

What it all meant was Blair's season—and career—at Arizona was over.

"It was difficult for me, because most people judged me without knowing what was going on," said Blair, the team's starting center. "I was not ineligible by UA or NCAA standards. People were saying, 'Joe is a lazy (person) and why didn't he give a shit? 'Well, at the time I had a two-year-old already. I'm in school trying to do this and do that, trying to see and be with my son as much as possible.

"My family (back home) is in a horrible financial situation, which no one thinks about."

Blair said he was using his $550 scholarship check to pay a number of things and was sending money home to help there, too.

"It took a toll on me," he said. "People asked, 'Why didn't I go to class?' Well, when you stay up with your son, it's tough. I also had practice, weights and basketball.

"I was already getting little rest to begin with. There were times I'd just say, (hell with it) and just go to sleep and miss class. Either do that, or I would not have made it through practice. But I'm not going to make excuses. People just judged me without knowing. I've moved on."

Things eventually turned out well for Blair. The Seattle Sonics drafted him in the second round, although he has not played in the NBA. He's played continuously in Europe, making a very comfortable life for himself and family.

"I don't regret anything, because I'm a better man because of the road I took," he said. "I don't think I'd be the man I am today if things would have come to me in a different way."

COME ON GUYS

You never would have expected it, but in that Stanford game where Arizona was getting beat and just not playing well overall, seldom- used guard Kelvin Eafon, who also played on the football team, lashed out at his team

It all came as a surprise to most everyone.

"He lit into the team like I've never seen any other player do," said Brett Hansen, the team's sports information director at the time.

Anything to get the players motivated, Eafon said.

"I was just disappointed because I knew we could play a whole lot better," said Eafon. "I just wanted them to understand how important it was to everybody and not just them. They needed to pick it up. I wanted to let them know the kind of opportunity they had."

Arizona won its next five games and eight of its next nine games.

"The guys did finally realize—in practice and in games—that if we straightened our act up we'd be playing well," Eafon said.

Chapter 10

1997 NCAA Title

Key Recruit Coming

There were high hopes for the 1996-97 season, although the reality of the whole season was that UA would be young—talented, but young.

Bringing some excitement to the team would be recruit Stephen Jackson, one of the better high school players in the country his senior season. He was joining Mike Bibby, Bennett Davison, Justin Wessel and Gene Edgerson as UA's incoming class. There was a problem, however. Jackson, after a number of attempts at passing the college entrance exam, failed to get into Arizona.

As it turned out, Arizona didn't need the talented Jackson, a six-foot-seven forward. Six months after failing to get into UA, Arizona won its NCAA title.

"We might not have won it had he arrived," said Simon, the leader of that team in 1997. "Our backcourt (and team) was already deep. We had Mike Bibby, Jason Terry, Mike Dickerson and me. Stephen and Michael would have shared that spot (small forward). And Steve was the type of player who would (have) demanded the ball and the shots. It would have changed (the team dynamics)."

Arizona coach Lute Olson feels otherwise. The addition of Jackson would have just helped the team be more athletic. It also would have helped when Simon was out for academic reasons the first semester.

"Stephen was a very flexible player who could play a number of positions," Olson said. "He would have encountered what other freshman typically encounter—learning to play with four other players because he had been a big scorer in high school. It would have helped us, because he would have given us another quality player. Our practices would have been better."

SCHOOL DAZE

School was never on the top of Miles Simon's list. Things have changed, in that he's returned to school to get his degree after finishing up his eligibility in 1998. But back when school should have been a priority, it wasn't.

It all came to light in news reports when he was declared academically ineligible the fall semester of his junior year. And it all came out the night Arizona traveled to Springfield, Massachusetts, to face North Carolina in the Hall of Fame Tip-Off Classic.

Originally, he was supposed to be out six games, but after the fall semester he still needed to pass a course in the winter session to become eligible.

It all came about because of a course change—and lack of seriousness in the classroom throughout his career—the summer before his junior season.

Miles Simon, who was named MVP of the 1997 Final Four, proved to be one of Arizona's all-time clutch players.

"I remember going to an instructor my sophomore year and asking to drop my class ... he was a cool teacher," Simon said. "He let me drop it, telling me I had to go to an academic advisor and ask if I needed a dean's signature. She said, 'No' that I didn't need one, and I was done."

Hardly. The drop in course created a chain of events that had him ineligible, which frustrated him to no end.

"I could have made it up in summer school and come back in the fall for workouts," he said. "We start practice, and I find out I can't play."

Simon then had to hustle to get back in good standing with the team. But it had to wait three more games after he failed to qualify after the fall semester.

"I needed a B in a class and got a C," he said. "I was five points short."

Simon eventually took additional classes during the second winter session to become eligible again.

Simon's grade problems—and his attempts to gain his eligibility—later came to light in a *Kansas City Star* report where it cited numerous steps UA took to keep Simon academically eligible. It even raised the suspicion that UA violated NCAA rules to keep him eligible.

Arizona officials said otherwise.

"Our office and the registrar's office looked at the (Simon matter) pretty aggressively when the allegations were brought to our attention, and we could not find any violation of NCAA or university rules," then UA attorney Michael Proctor said.

Simon eventually sued the school, the *Kansas City Star* and others for violating his right to privacy when it came to grades, which are protected under the Family Education Rights and Privacy Act of 1994.

Simon's case eventually was dismissed.

HE'S LEAVING—MAYBE

It was such a tough time for Simon sitting out the first semester—having to go through academic problems—that late into December, just a week or two before he'd become eligible again, Simon wanted to transfer.

And ironically it was to Utah, the same school that knocked UA out of the NCAAs a season later.

"I really was considering it," he said. "That semester I felt (betrayed). I spoke to my dad and he was good friends with (then-assistant coach) Donny Daniels. I was frustrated at Arizona."

The problem for Simon, however, was that he had only two days to decide what to do, because Utah was about to begin its classes.

"Coach Olson sat me down and said that the guys wanted me on this team," Simon said. "But I had to step it up in the classroom, telling me this and that. He told me, 'This is your team, but it's your responsibility to get things done. It's all on you.' I figured it was, and that I needed to get things straight."

THE WEAZE HOBBLES THROUGH

Arizona was loaded with young talent to begin the 1996-97 season. Emphasis on young. One freshman was Justin Wessel, who had potential but was thin at 6-8, 210 pounds. He was being considered for a possible redshirt season. Through the season's first six games he didn't play, then he suffered a broken ankle in what was called an "off-the-court" incident. He actually broke it while falling off Mike Bibby's car after deciding to ride a short distance on the hood.

While traveling with the team to Detroit for a game against Michigan, Wessel was on crutches going through the airport.

"To see him hobbling around on crutches through a crowded O'Hare Airport while carrying a huge stuffed Minnie Mouse doll was priceless," said Brett Hansen.

But apparently necessary. The doll was for his then-girlfriend back in Iowa.

"I had won it while we were in the Wooden Classic in California, playing pop-a-shot at Disneyland," Wessel said. "Along with the doll I had a full load of wash to take back to my mom. I had to get a wheelchair because I couldn't walk with everything. I got on and just rolled through the airport. It was crazy."

He's Crazy

Midway through the season, Arizona's Davison was dared to do something a bit crazy, in part because that's who he was and what he did. Some UA players dared him to ride on the luggage conveyor belt at the Eugene, Oregon, airport. Not wanting to seem like a wimp, Davison took the challenge.

"That was Bennett," Wessell said. "He'd do something like that on a regular basis. It was one of those things where you challenge someone and say, 'You won't do that, because you're scared to do it.' But he did it. He's the only one on the team that would have done that."

Bennett went through twice.

"The airport people didn't see it," Wessel said.

A SMASHING SUCCESS

A.J. Bramlett, one of the best and well-mannered players to come to UA, had been criticized for not being aggressive or being strong while being the team's center. On February 18, 1997, that all changed. In practice, he shattered the backboard on an attempted dunk. He suffered cuts to his left arm that required stitches, but he gained some confidence and some bravado from the experience.

"A.J. was never a very confident player, but his chest sort of puffed out that day he broke the backboard," Olson said. "One of the best people for AJ was JT. Jason was always beaming with confidence, and JT did a good job of getting AJ to get his self-image to where he needed it to be in becoming a very good player."

When Olson recruited Bramlett, it was the first time he sat down with four parents.

There was his mom, his stepdad, his dad and his stepmom.

"Everything was decided by committee," Olson said. "It was good to get him away from home and have him hang with somebody. JT was perfect."

The two became fast friends.

"We clicked from day one," Terry said. "We had played in an all-star game in Albuquerque together."

When the two arrived on campus to begin their college careers, by coincidence they ran into each other at a local store.

"We were looking for stuff to put in our dorm room," Terry said. "We had picked out the same bed spread and bed sheets. Amazing. We kind of clicked from there."

LOCKER-ROOM TROUBLES

Arizona had just been swept by the Bay area schools and it didn't look all that great for the Wildcats heading into the NCAA tournament the next week. Although they lost in close games to Stanford (81-80) and California (79-77), there was plenty of tension in the postgame locker room in the season-finale against Cal.

Soon after UA lost, assistant coach Phil Johnson singled out a couple of players for the loss—and they didn't even play.

"He went after the entire scout team," said Ryan Hansen. "That was a stressful time. We were 19-9 and had just been swept. He needed a scapegoat. And he's a passionate dude."

But so was one of Johnson's targets. Quynn Tebbs, a 21-year-old redshirt freshman. An argument ensued.

"Quynn felt it was an attack on his work ethic," Hansen said. "Everyone was just stressed out. Coach O just squashed it, saying we had other things to think about."

KEY GAME

Some might argue, but one of the most crucial games in the NCAA tournament for UA was the first-round game with South Alabama.

Arizona looked beat 33 minutes into the game. Arizona was down 53-43 with seven minutes left, and it looked bleak with the Jaguars stifling UA's high-scoring offense with a tough zone defense.

"I had a horrible feeling with seven minutes left," said Brett Hansen, remembering he was thumbing through the media guide to see what records were being set in another possible first-round loss. "I was almost sick to my stomach and was wondering how long a Greyhound Bus trip back Tucson would take as opposed to being on the team flight."

Terry, with a game-high five steals, changed UA's fortune helping UA go on a 22-4 run in the final minutes to get the win.

"I just was not going to lose, no way," Terry said. "I'd do whatever—if it meant fouling out to get us back in, I'd do it. I got real aggressive on the ball.

"That was THE game. As everyone knows, it's the first game that usually gives us trouble. If you can get past that first one and then the second one, then there's a chance you can win it. I wasn't really scared. We had nothing to lose, because it was either move on or go home and live out the summer. We moved on. I had the five steals and was on top of the world—what a feeling."

ID PLEASE

This would have never passed in today's world of high security at the nation's airports, but after the first and second rounds of the 1997 NCAA Tournament in Memphis, Arizona players attempted to board a plane to head home. The team encountered a problem when standout guard Mike Bibby didn't have his identification.

In UA's attempt to prove who he was, Ryan Hansen, the team's director of basketball operations, tracked down the team's sports information man, Brett Hansen, in order to get a media guide.

"I showed the ticketing agent the guide and his picture on his bio page," Brett Hansen said, "and they submitted him a ticket."

Mike Bibby solidified Arizona as Point Guard University after just two years in Tucson.

KNOCKOUT WIN

A little-known fact about Arizona basketball is it was the last school to hand former North Carolina coach Dean Smith a loss. At the 1997 Final Four, Arizona defeated North Carolina 66-58 in the semifinals in Indianapolis.

Five months later, after a glorious Hall of Fame career, Smith surprisingly called it quits just before the 1997-98 season.

Arizona's Olson and Smith have long been good friends.

"He's always been a great gentleman and such an innovator as far as basketball is concerned," Olson said, of Smith. "It was just a thrill to have a chance to play against his team in the playoffs. I've always admired him. In fact, a number of things we did were taken from him. He was one of my coaching heroes. There's three: Coach John Wooden, Coach Pete Newell and Dean Smith."

For his career, Olson went 3-1 against Smith, beating him twice in the NCAA tournament.

THE NOTE

While Arizona was making its improbable run to the 1997 title, Simon made mention of a letter North Carolina coach Dean Smith sent to him while Simon was being recruited in the early 1990s.

"I got it my junior year, and it said he was going to stop recruiting me but that he liked how I played," Simon said. "They were going to stop recruiting me, because they already had two guards at the shooting guard spot already."

The two guards were Donald Williams and Dante Calebria—two players who had helped Smith win a national title in 1993.

"He just wanted to wish me the best of luck in my career," Simon said of the letter's contents. "He knew I'd be a success no matter where I went, but that he didn't want to over recruit at one position."

Simon still has the letter because he loved Carolina. In college, he kept the letter posted on a board in his room.

Simon had intended to take the letter with him while UA was to face North Carolina at the Final Four but forgot it at home.

"In the midst of the hoopla I just left it," he said. "I was going to play with it while it was in my shoe or sock."

As it turned out, UA was the last team to beat a North Carolina team led by Dean Smith. Simon still talks about that.

"I tell people that all the time—that I beat Dean Smith in his last college game ever," Simon said. "And I beat Rick Pitino. I think about that a lot."

Soon after losing to UA in the NCAA title game, Pitino quit to become the Boston Celtics head coach. He's now with the Louisville Cardinals.

THE GEEKY FAN

During Arizona's run to the NCAA Final Four and eventual NCAA title, none other than child actor Jaleel White, better known as *Family Matters'* Steve Urkel, showed up supporting Arizona. He did have a history of following Arizona when he wasn't following his UCLA Bruins. There was no better place than to bandwagon on the Cats at the Final Four in Indianapolis. On one occasion, he spent time with the team playing video games in their hotel rooms.

"He came to our summer camps," Olson said, of the connection. "He'd been to the Duke camps, too. In camp, we had to isolate him in the dorm so he stayed with Matthew (his grandson) on the coach's floor so as to not cause a scene because of all the autograph requests. But that's when he became a fan."

While in Indianapolis, he was even more popular than Olson.

"We were at a restaurant in Indianapolis and he and his group see us and join us, but because there are too many people they sit at another table," Olson said. "People would walk by, give double takes and then come in and ask for autographs."

WHITE HOUSE EXPERIENCE

One of the perks of winning an NCAA title is getting to visit the White House, being allowed to meet and greet the president. Arizona experienced it in November of 1997.

"This is what it's all about," said UA's Gene Edgerson, an aspiring teacher.

It turned out to be a 24-hour whirlwind tour. First there was the meeting with President Clinton and Vice President Gore and presenting Clinton with an Arizona uniform.

Then there was the four-hour tour of Washington, D.C. where Arizona senator Jim Kolbe played tour guide.

"Visiting the White House was a lot of fun," said Olson, a registered independent. "It was well organized, because we got so much done in a day."

As for meeting Clinton and Gore, Olson said, "The thing that was most impressive was how personable both President Clinton and Vice President Gore were. With Vice President Gore, I had always thought in watching him that he didn't seem like he was that warm and personable, yet when you meet him face to face, you walk away with that impression. That was the biggest surprise I had. I didn't expect to see him so outgoing and as friendly as he was."

It Suits You

Jason Terry was particularly happy to be heading to see the president. In part because he was able to buy a new suit for the occasion. Terry was proud of it, too. As he boarded the plane he declared, "Yo, everybody, check out my draft day outfit."

There was one problem. He was wearing white socks with it.

MVP Time

Simon had a glorious run during the NCAA tournament, but he really stood out during the Final Four. He scored 54 points in UA's two games, going 17 for 37 from the floor. In the title game against Kentucky, he had 30 points, 14 of which came from the free throw line where he went 14 for 17.

"For me, it was a dream—an ultimate feeling," Simon said. "I had been to a number of Final Fours and watched a number, too. It was amazing how we got there and how I played. I could not have imagined it being any better.

It all ended in what will forever be etched into Wildcat fans' minds and will forever be part of UA basketball history: Simon clutching the game ball as he fell to the floor at the RCA Dome in Indianapolis. The image has long been known as the moment UA officially won the title in 1997.

"I couldn't believe it," said Simon, who has a picture of it at home in Los Angeles. "When I caught the ball in the game's final seconds and they didn't foul me ... we actually had done it. We won it all. It's just an amazing feeling."

Sparkplug Jason Terry, high socks and all, became player of the year in 1999. The reward for his efforts: a new suit "for draft day."

R-E-V-E-N-G-E

Little did anyone know it, but the 1996 meeting against Kansas, where UA lost 83-80 in Denver, was going to have an impact a year later in the NCAA tournament. Arizona, with a relatively young team with no senior starter, and Kansas, 34-1, was ranked No. 1 going into the tournament. Yet, despite being a 10-point underdog, Arizona was confident it could beat Kansas.

"I'll never forget when someone asked Michael Dickerson how they felt being the underdog," Olson said. "Mike was like, 'Underdog?' He was shocked that somebody had Kansas favored over us. They were confident they could beat Kansas."

And all because of the close game the year before.

"It wasn't a case of us being in awe of Kansas as you might think it might be," said Olson, of that 1997 game when many thought KU was invincible. "And maybe that might have been the case had we not played them before."

And nearly won.

"We knew we could match up with them," said Simon. "They returned the same team, and we thought we were better. I knew we could play with them, because we should have beaten them the season before. We jumped on them like no other team had before (that season)."

It didn't come without a struggle. Arizona had a 75-62 lead with 3:28 left, only to see Kansas storm back with an 11-0 run. But on three attempts to tie the game in the final seconds, Kansas came up short.

"Kansas was in shock that the little guys had shot down the big guys," Simon said.

BOYS ON THE BUS

How big was UA's game against Kentucky for the NCAA title? Former UA All-American Sean Elliott and teammate Jud Buechler made the game. While there, Elliott felt he had to let UA players know what the title meant to him, speaking to them on the team bus before it left for the game.

"I didn't even know if they would listen," Elliott said. "I wasn't sure if the speech would go over or effect them or inspire them. But I told them they were as good as Kentucky, as good as anybody, and that this was a once-in-a-lifetime opportunity to leave everything on the floor because we were all pulling for them."

The speech hit home for everyone.

"It was big, because Sean was saying you have to win it for everybody," Simon said. "And that you have to take advantage of the opportunity because you might not get there again. You can't take it for granted that even though we're all coming back next year, and we had a possibility of winning it next year. We had to win it now when the chance is put in front of you."

CATS VS. CATS

If Arizona were to beat Kentucky it would make history, becoming the first No. 4 seed to win the title by going through three No. 1 seeds. Arizona was the underdog—again. But they didn't mind it because they had worked hard and played hard in the role of an underdog. It gave the Wildcats added motivation.

"Kentucky was scared of us," Simon said. "When we saw that they didn't start in the halfcourt press, we knew we had them. I'm not sure if they were afraid of our guards—me, JT, Mike Bibby. We just made it hard for them to press us.

"What we ended up doing was trying to attack their big men. Eventually when they went to the press, it didn't bother us all night," Simon said.

EXCUSE ME, MISS

One day while having lunch, Mike Bibby, John Ash, Josh Pastner and Miles Simon were at a table waiting for their food when Pastner excused himself to go to the restroom. Knowing this was a chance to have fun at the expense of the ever-serious Pastner, the other three decided to put some Sprite into Pastner's water while he was gone, figuring Pastner would never know.

In his lifetime, Pastner has never had a carbonated beverage of any kind.

But upon Pastner's return the guys were just too nonchalant about things so Pastner knew something was up. It just didn't feel right.

"We're at the table just sitting there all quiet," Simon recalled, "and Josh looks around at all three of us, and says, 'Excuse me miss, can I get a new water?' He didn't even taste it. He suspected we had done something."

BET YOU

Seemingly there isn't a season that goes by, and Josh Pastner is talking national championship. It doesn't matter the circumstances.

Back in 1996-97 when Pastner was a freshman, he—along with Ash and Bennett Davison—made a bet with Simon, saying that if they won the NCAA title Pastner would have to drink a soda and the other two would have to get tattoos. At the time, Simon was in the process of getting his second or third one.

Pastner said, "It would be worth it" to drink a soda if they won it all. Small price, right?

Not exactly.

Arizona—surprisingly won the title that season—and Simon is still waiting to collect on his bet.

"As soon as we won the title none of the guys gets a tattoo, and Josh still hasn't had a soda," Simon said. "We can't get guys to follow through with their bets."

SIGN WHERE?

To say the Arizona program has come a long way from the early years of Olson and the one and only year of Ben Lindsey is an exaggeration. But in recent years, Arizona players have become mini-celebrities, not only in Tucson, but throughout the country, particularly on game day.

It's not rare to see fans from other schools sit around hotel lobbies waiting to get autographs on basketballs, pennants and shoes. But during Arizona's run to a potential repeat title in 1998—it would have been the first for a team since Duke did it in 1991, '92—Arizona players were almost rock-star like.

"I signed breasts, thighs, stomachs, everything," said Simon. "It was crazy."

Cap Caper

Upon arriving home to McKale Center after beating Providence for the right to got to the Final Four in 1997, Arizona players were greeted by a few thousand fans.

So when the players began to greet them on the floor, someone swiped a New York Yankees hat—his brother-in-law Darryl Strawberry played for the World Champion Yankees—from Simon's backpack.

"That was my favorite cap," Simon said. "I didn't know it was gone until I got back to my apartment after the ceremony. I thought it was lost and gone for good."

Not exactly.

Nearly a year later in the middle of his senior season, Simon said, "the hat showed up in my locker. I don't know where it came from."

Simon promptly tossed it in the garbage.

"There wasn't anything on it," Simon said, "but I threw it away, because I didn't know who wore it. I didn't want it."

Hotel Paradise

There were about 200 to 300 people in the hotel lobby waiting for the team to return from the RCA Dome after winning the NCAA. The lobby smelled of cigar smoke, beer and everything that goes along with a celebration.

"It smelled like a frat house," said Brett Hansen. "As soon as the fans saw the players, I realized what it must have been like to travel with the Beatles."

Upon arriving to the hotel, the team knew it had no chance of going through the main lobby to get in. So UA officials decided to take the team through the back door.

"I felt like a rock star—and I've never felt like that since," said Terry, now in his sixth season as an NBA player. "That was the greatest feeling ever."

HEEERE'S LUTE

No sooner had Olson gotten back home from Indianapolis after winning the title did he get a call from NBC asking if he'd be a guest on *The Tonight Show with Jay Leno* in Los Angeles.

The usually stoic Olson surprisingly said yes, heading to the show to be among guests Clint Black and former *NYPD Blue* actress Kim Delaney.

David Letterman's producers also called, but Olson preferred to do something closer to home rather than go to New York.

"It was fun," Olson said. "The most difficult part of it was waiting in the dressing room and not knowing when you'd go on. I was the last guy on. It was a long wait."

While on, Olson, and his perfect coif, got some ribbing, with Leno giving him a can of "Lute Spray" a hairspray product.

"Wouldn't you like to have that hair?" Leno asked the audience.

Olson still has the "Lute Spray" can somewhere in his home, safely tucked away as a memento.

CAN WE TALK?

A month after winning the title, Arizona embarked on a three-week trip to Australia. Most of the players didn't want to go.

It already had been a long season. Midway through the trip the players wanted to go home. They were tired. They wanted to enjoy their fruits of a championship. Michael Dickerson already had left for the states, saying he needed to be with his ailing grandmother.

A day or so later, the other players got together to see if they could try to convince Olson to end the trip.

"We were in Melbourne, and I got a call from JT to try to meet with Coach O after he came back from dinner," Simon said.

So some of the players were told to wait in the hotel lobby for Olson. They waited and waited and waited.

"We waited a few hours; he and Bobbi came in real late," Simon said. "I said, 'Coach, me and some of the guys want to talk to you.'"

Olson instructed them to go to his room in 10 minutes.

"We all sat down and the first thing he said was, 'Going home is not an option,'" Simon said. "All the guys' faces dropped. That was the only thing we wanted to talk to him about. He shot it down and then said, 'Is there anything else?'"

Olson knew there wasn't.

Simon had to think fast, saying perhaps the guys could get better NCAA title rings. Olson said maybe, but that he'd have to check the budget.

Simon quickly replied, "We already did, and we have money."

Olson approved the new rings.

"That was the only good thing to come out of the meeting," Simon said, laughing.

TOUGH GUY COMPETITION

On the Australia trip, Arizona went to a youth correctional facility to play a group of teenagers who were locked up for various reasons. It was to be a goodwill gesture on UA's part.

It was a maximum security facility for troubled children. It also was the last place anyone wanted to be. To make it more competitive, just the freshmen played—Mike Bibby, Josh Paster, Gene Edgerson, Justin Wessel and Quynn Tebbs.

"I was so mad because I didn't want anything to do with that," Wessel said. "It was one of those things were you're playing a bunch of five-foot guys, and it's the greatest thing in the world to them."

Wessel and Edgerson wanted to play the game without having to jump.

"We were so much bigger than them," Wessel said. "And we had all the other guys (UA players) cheering for the other team; they were rooting against us."

There may have been a reason.

"We asked one of the guys what he was in for, and no one would say," Wessel said.

Added Edgerson: "I know a couple of guys were scared. I was one of the few that wasn't. Josh was so terrified. He was like, 'What if they foul us? What if we foul them? What if there is a fight?' He was scared."

Arizona eventually won. As UA was about to leave the facility they were taken through a long hallway and were later informed that the guys they just played against were in for committing crimes that were almost unbelievable. Killings, rapes, robberies.

"One guy says, 'That guy over there slit his mom's throat.' I got chills when he said that. I just played against the guy and was sweating on him and bumping the guy, and he's in for killing his mom? Had I known that I would have been a whole lot nicer," Wessel said.

Chapter 11

2000s

En Garde II

They weren't exactly the second coming of Reeves and Stoudamire, but they may have had just as much an impact. Even if it was just for two years.

The two also had a nickname: Batman and Robin.

Freshmen Jason Gardner and Gilbert Arenas helped Arizona continue the school's success in the backcourt. The two helped the Wildcats gain a No. 1 seed in the West in 2000 and a championship game appearance against Duke in 2001.

"Had they stayed together, who knows?," said Olson, when asked if they could have rivaled Reeves and Stoudamire as his best backcourt ever. "As sophomores, they were the best pair out there."

Just two weeks after losing to Duke in the Final Four in 2001, Arenas declared for the NBA.

The popular Gene Edgerson was admired for his hustle and candor. (Brian Bahr/Getty Images)

I'll Get You

It had to be one of the funnier moments in McKale Center that season of 2001, when Arizona was chasing an NCAA title and there was a mixed bag of personalities.

Before practice one day, Gene Edgerson spent the day chasing Arenas around McKale Center after the young and carefree Arenas let the air out of Edgerson's tires earlier in the day.

At the time, Edgerson, a serious senior, wanted to kill Arenas.

"I laugh about that all the time," said Edgerson. "Gilbert was irritating me one day, and I wanted to strangle him. I was older, wiser, and Gilbert was so immature. And here I am supposed to be mature and everything and he got deep into my skin."

They can laugh about it now. Actually, they laughed about it then, too.

"Coach (Olson) walked onto the court and asked, 'What's Gilbert doing up there in the stands?' And (associate head coach Jim) Roz (Rosborough) tolds Lute that Gene wanted to kill Gilbert," then-assistant Jay John said.

"Lute says, 'After 30 years in the business you should be able to handle the situation, don't you think?' Roz said, 'Yes.' Well then, Lute says, get him down here."

UA survived another practice—and there was no death.

That's Mr. Wright to You

Michael Wright didn't say much, and when he did, people listened. One instance during his sophomore year points it out. It was early 1999, and the players were beginning to play in the annual pickup games. And with Jason Gardner and Gilbert

Arenas being freshmen—and feeling they had something to prove—decided they'd run and gun every time down the court. It clearly wasn't the right thing to do—especially being freshmen.

"They were just jacking up shots, but in not so many words, Mike pulled them aside and said, 'You will never do that again. You pass the ball to me every time,'" recalled Ryan Hansen. "They listened to him."

MICHAEL OLSON, POWER FORWARD

While Wright was at Arizona, he didn't say much. And when he did it was very infrequent and in hushed tones.

By the end of his career—he stayed only three seasons—he was not only known for his aggressive power moves to the basket but his nickname "Michael Olson."

His teammates called him that because it was rare that Olson ever got on him.

Said Wright: "They tease me about it."

But there was a reason why Olson admired Wright: he worked hard all the time.

"You never heard Michael say anything other than saying it was his fault (when he messed up)," said Olson. "They could throw a lousy pass to him but Michael would take the blame. He'd never point the finger at someone.

"He came to practice and worked his butt off every day. He wanted to be coached, be faced with constructive criticism. No way was he going to take it personally. And that was from the first day of practice."

FAST FRIENDS

Richard Jefferson and Walton's friendship—and ties that will forever bind them—happened long before Jefferson was injured and Walton replaced him in their freshmen season. The two became fast friends early in the recruiting process when the two—along with Ricky Anderson—visited UA. Here was this dichotomy. Walton, who had every reason to be loud and flamboyant being the son of basketball great Bill Walton, was quiet and reserved. Jefferson, albeit one of the state's best high school players, was loud and fun-loving. Apparently, opposites attract.

"It all started on that visit," said Jefferson. "We didn't know much about each other before that. But we liked hanging out with one another. Funny thing was that we thought one of us would go to UCLA, Arizona, Utah or New Mexico. There was no way the three (Anderson, too) top forwards in the West would go to the same school. But it ended up happening."

First, Walton committed. Jefferson found out and then committed. A couple of weeks later Anderson committed.

But it was Walton and Jefferson who were seemingly inseparable. Walton could take Jefferson's one-liners. He could take his bravado. Walton was the ying to Jefferson's yang.

When Jefferson suffered that stress fracture against Stanford, the Walton's joked that he had officially become a Walton. The foot problems made it official.

Now, they will be friends forever.

"He's one of the major reasons why I got through that first year," said Walton. "He was always positive. He was just a good friend who I could talk to. Now, we speak to one another about two times a week. The college years are the best times of your life, because that's when you meet some of your best friends."

NCAA DOESN'T LIKE FRIENDS

The summer of 2000, Bill Walton invited Jefferson to attend son Christopher's graduation and later the NBA finals between Los Angeles and Indianapolis. Walton was working the game as analyst for NBC.

Jefferson visited the Waltons three times that summer with Bill paying for Jefferson's trip home all three times. But that's a no-no according to the NCAA. It constitutes extra benefits.

"Obviously," Olson said, "if Bill Walton knew this were a violation, he would not have allowed it to happen. But if you ask me, they ought to throw away the NCAA rule book and write a new one, with the first rule being: common sense."

Jefferson had to repay the NCAA $400 for the things Walton provided. He also had to sit out UA's game against St. Mary's.

"Richard was OK with it," said Luke. "Richard takes things well. And we beat St. Mary's by 70 (101-41). My dad was just crushed over it. He still apologizes for it. But to Rich it wasn't that big of a deal."

Well, not exactly. At the time, Jefferson couldn't believe he had to go through all that just to be with a friend—almost family by this time.

"The NCAA is a bunch of crooks," Jefferson said. "They make so much money off of athletes in football, basketball and baseball. I understand they have a job to do, but it's the way they do those things. It's not right. To say that your teammate can't invite you to his house or go somewhere is wrong. Then to have to pay back tickets?"

High-flyer Richard Jefferson had his troubles with the NCAA, but opponents also had plenty of trouble with him.

CLASSIC STUFF

The team's end-of-the-season dinners are usually fun times. A week before the start of the 2001 NCAA tournament, it was one to remember. Jefferson, ever the cocky cutup, was in classic form. When it came to exchanging gifts with roommates, Jefferson proved to be the comical hit. Just as he was the year before when he gave Walton an autographed picture of himself.

"That's just how Richard is," said Walton. "He gave me the picture so that one day I could show my family that I played with him and that I knew him."

In 2001, he gave Walton a video full of highlights—all involving Jefferson. You know, Jefferson said, just in case they think the picture isn't real or in case he loses the picture.

Of course, not to be outdone, Walton give Richard a plane ticket stub (remember the suspension) so he could visit him any time.

"That just showed the relationship we had," Jefferson said. "We were great friends."

ROSBOROUGH TAKES OVER

It was easily one of the team's toughest times. Olson had just turned over the reins to associate head coach Jim Rosborough after his wife of 47 years, Bobbi, was gravely ill with ovarian cancer. The team was still in a state of flux from a not-so-impressive early part of the season.

To say things were down and melancholy would be an understatement. But Rosborough, who has been with Olson for more than 20 seasons, did what he had to to keep the team focused. First and foremost, he told the guys he was in charge. And the guys respected him for that.

"It wasn't so much Roz being the coach, but it was about all of us getting through it all," said Jefferson. "Roz was as close as anyone to Bobbi—perhaps closest outside of Coach Olson. For him not to be able to go through his own grieving process (was unfortunate). He probably needed his time away, too. But he sucked it up and was there for us. He knew we were a bunch of young men who needed to be guided."

BOBBI REMEMBERED

If there was one thing Jefferson possessed—outside of great leaping and athletic ability—it was the gift to speak in front of an audience. He had his chance at the public memorial at McKale Center, honoring Bobbi just days after her passing on January 1, 2001.

He was eloquent and insightful.

"That was tough," he said. "But to be able to represent my teammates, that was something very special. We did that and then we had to go and play just a day and a half later. For a lot of us that was our first introduction into the world."

OLSON RETURNS

After Bobbi Olson passed on New Year's Day of 2001, Olson understandably took time off to be with his family. The biggest question bantered about was: when was Olson going to return to the team, one already struggling through tough times with an 8-4 record? After all, many thought this was the best team in the country.

After two weeks and a 3-1 record without him, Olson returned on Monday after UA's trip to Washington. He didn't decide to return until that morning, after speaking with family members.

"They're all going back to work," Olson said. "We just felt the biggest problem for me was having too much time on my own to be by myself."

What really did it was his talk with daughter Vicki who said, "Mom would have wanted you to go back, so you need to go back."

But the times rarely got easier for Olson, who was married to Bobbi for 47 years. The alone times at home were the toughest.

"It hits you and makes you sick to your stomach," Olson said. "But in talking with people who have been in similar situations, it'll feel like you're having an out-of-body experience. It just hits you. It could be driving in the car or sitting at home. I don't think it'll go away."

RJ, THE DEFENDER

Much had been made of Richard Jefferson's athletic abilities throughout his career at Arizona. As Brett Hansen, the team's former sports information man, said, "Richard is Vince Carter with a jump shot."

But he was so much more, also. Throughout his junior season, Jefferson became more and more of a defensive stopper. And he thrived on it. If scoring wasn't an option—or if he had a bad night—he'd turn to his defense.

"Coach Olson kind of put me out there, saying Richard Jefferson could be a defensive stopper for us," Jefferson said, of that 2000-2001 season. "Not wanting Coach Olson to look like a liar, I focused on defense. He told me that every time we went to the Final Four we had a defensive stopper—Reggie Geary, Jason Terry or Michael Dickerson. We always had someone we could count on. He put me out there, and I tried to make it happen."

At no point in his college career did it become more apparent than in Arizona's game against Illinois in the Elite Eight in San Antonio. Illinois's Frank Williams, after scorching Kansas for 30 in the Sweet 16 the game before, had to deal with Jefferson, a just-as-strong player with perhaps more athletic ability. Remember that Williams had 27 points in a game against UA six months earlier in Maui.

"Coach thought that would help change up the game," said Jefferson. "It was to put someone taller on him and disrupt him."

Williams went three for 15 from the field in UA's 87-81 victory over Illinois to advance to the Final Four.

"Everything will be magnified at the bigger stage," said Jefferson, who by now was being regarded as UA's main defender. "After Williams had a big game the game before, Coach Olson prepped me. He wanted to use my athletic ability."

WALTON HURT

Just two days before Arizona was headed to its fourth Final Four, Walton was injured. He caught his right thumb—his shooting hand—on Arenas's jersey in practice. He suffered a stress fracture but could still play. He played 16 minutes against the Spartans and another 16 against Duke in the title game.

"That was a tough one," said Walton. "We had a great team that year, and the injury hurt the team. It's tough because you wait and play your whole career to get to the Final Four and something like that happens. It was just a freak accident. I couldn't do much with it."

Walton was able to play after UA officials shot it for the pain. "I couldn't feel my hand on that side," he said. "I didn't have a good touch with it. It was awful."

He went two for seven from the field at the Final Four.

DOOKIE VITALE

As Arizona was making its run to the Final Four and eventual national championship game, all the rage and talk was about Duke. Duke this, Duke that. But Arizona was pretty good, too. One of those promoting Duke heavily was ESPN analyst Dick Vitale, who seemingly always has Duke on the tip of his lips, trumpeting its praises.

Arizona coach Lute Olson had heard enough.

"Our guys get tired of hearing Dookie Vitale talk," Olson quipped in a rare one-liner from the usually straightforward coach.

The media had a blast with it. And so did Olson. He said it a number of times. But it couldn't have been his line. Right? It wasn't. Olson's humor is a more dry wit.

"It was Billy Baffert who popped it off," admitted Olson, referring to the brother of famed horse trainer Bob Baffert.

"Dick didn't particularly agree with it," Olson said. "He is definitely the salesperson for Duke, and rightfully so. Plus he's going to push the teams that are on ESPN a lot."

Actually, Vitale had no problem with it.

"I just thought it was great," Vitale said. "It was cute as hell."

But he still had Duke winning the title that year in 2001.

"What's not to praise about Duke?" he asked. "Nine Final Fours in 16 years. Back-to-back titles. Come on!"

DUKE WINS

Arizona was three minutes away from winning its second national title, having a chance to beat a very good Duke team. But with the Blue Devils' Mike Dunleavy hitting key three-pointers in a 45-second span to help give Duke a 10-point cushion, Arizona was second best.

But the Cats played perhaps as well as it could have. Walton was hurt; Gilbert was hurt the game before, suffering from shoulder and chest pains after a collision.

"I knew going into the game that we were in a bit of trouble because of Luke's injury, and Gilbert couldn't participate in Sunday's workout," said Olson. "He (Arenas) couldn't lift his hand over his shoulder. And when you looked at what our options were, well, we just didn't have any options."

Arizona played close, despite some grumbling from the crowd that Duke was getting special treatment from the referees. It wasn't until Duke took a 10-point lead late in the game that Arizona was out of it. Four UA players scored in double figures, with Loren Woods (22 points, 11 rebounds) and Michael Wright (10 points, 11 rebounds) having double-doubles.

"I knew we'd have to have solid efforts from everybody because of the injuries," said Olson. "We were right there. Loren had a great game and the others did step up. Had Luke not had that injury, we wouldn't have had to play Gilbert as much. We just didn't have many options."

NO DOOM AND GLOOM

Just a week after Arizona had made it back to its second NCAA title game in four seasons, Arizona fans had to come to grips with the reality of losing a non-senior player or two to the NBA. Earlier in the season, Olson was resigned to the fact that he'd lose at least one player to the NBA. Was it going to be junior Wright, who had a stellar first half of the season but a so-so second half? Was it going to be junior Jefferson, who was as talented as any player in the nation but still unproven? Or was it going to be talented yet young Arenas?

In a matter of days, all three declared for the NBA—never to return as UA players. But soon after—in a press conference talking about the season ahead and what just happened—Olson promptly told everyone, "there will be no doom and gloom in the program. Arizona was good before and will be good after the player defections.

"I've long said that worrying is like being in a rocking chair—it keeps you busy, but it doesn't get you anywhere," Olson said. "I don't worry about things I can't control. If a guy decides he's ready to go and has thought things through, well all you can do is support his decision. It can't be a case where you think he's made a mistake and you do this or that to try to make him stay."

BOBBI AND LUTE OLSON COURT

In the spring of 2000, Arizona officials decided it was time to honor Olson, by naming the court Lute Olson Court.

The family had gotten word that Bobbi, after nearly a two-year battle with ovarian cancer, had gone into remission, and everyone thought that it would be appropriate to honor Olson for his success at UA.

Almost a year later, the University changed the name to Lute and Bobbi Olson Court, shortly after her death.

"It was a no-brainer to include her," said Livengood. "With so many things to think about, and in my own hindsight I wish I would have thought about it the first time. It was the right thing to do. She was a major part of this program. It needed to be done."

The players—current and past—said it was appropriate that she be included, in part because she recruited them as much as Lute did. She was famous for her cinnamon pancakes. The calming voice when Olson was getting on them. She was everything to the program.

"I know I might offend some people, but it's something that I should have done from the beginning," Livengood said.

MAKE A BET

During Arizona's tip to Australia there was more than basketball being played. Some Arizona players had fun at the casinos. One place was Melbourne, home of the Crown Entertainment Complex, which is billed as the world's largest casino.

"Isaiah and I have this impression that roulette is the easiest game in the casino," said Jason Ranne. "We sit down and figure it's a 50-50 chance to win. So we bet black. We lose. So we double it the next time.

"We lose again. I don't want to do it anymore, but Isaiah talks me into it. I throw down another $100, so in 15 minutes I'm down something like $300."

But he's not done. Realizing he might not be playing the game that suits him, he and Isaiah move to the blackjack table.

"It's a new game," he said.

Same results. He lost another $100.

"Everyone was wining money except me and Isaiah," Ranne said. "Luck never changed."

Soon after, he was on the phone to his father, Richard, a cardiac surgeon, to wire money.

"If you want me to eat, send money," Ranne joked. "I had money in my account, so I was more kidding when I called my parents."

GARDNER + H$_2$0 = TROUBLE

Jason Gardner isn't one for being on or in water, but in Australia he was part of a crew that went to see the Great Barrier Reef.

"I slept through it, because I didn't want to get sick," he said. "The second time I woke up and one of the lady diving instructors had to take my hand and jump off the boat with me. Everyone went nuts after that."

Then there was the time when the guide picked up a sea cucumber "and made me touch it. It was gross."

DON'T SHOOT!

It was to have been a festive occasion with Lute Olson being honored for being named into the Naismith Hall of Fame. But the Northern Arizona game turned out to be more than that. In fact, Olson seemingly had never been more upset—even if Arizona had easily disposed of NAU, 101-66, in McKale Center.

Olson's ire was directed at walk-on Fil Torres, who hit a last-second three-pointer just moments after Olson had instructed his players to sit on the lead and let the clock run out, a show of kindness and respect for the other team.

"That was in poor taste," Olson said, of the shot. "I had told them no shot. If he's not listening, he's telling me that he doesn't want to play the next few games."

Problem was—Torres didn't hear Olson give the instructions, and he was hearing more than 14,000 fans yell at him to shoot so he could register his first career points.

"I never thought I'd make it," Torres said. "But I could see why he didn't want it. But at the same time all my teammates and everybody wanted me to. By the reaction you could tell everyone wanted it."

Torres chalked it up as a learning experience. A few days later he went into Olson's office to offer up an apology for his actions.

"He wasn't that upset, no more than when someone messes up when they don't listen to what he says," Torres said. "He gets mad if you don't listen. You see him upset before. But I just said, yes, I messed up. My bad."

Yet, according to Richard Paige, the team's spokesman, Olson was beyond mad. "He was livid," Paige said. "Livid.

"He was as upset with that single play as anything as I've seen in my time here at UA," Paige said. "It's rare where Lute will say something like 'Don't shoot' to a player and they won't listen. Next thing you know Fil is pulling up from the logo (about 25 feet from the basket)."

Paige feels that had Olson not had a ceremony to celebrate his induction right after the game, Torres would have been off the team that very day.

"I never thought that," Torres said.

Chapter 12

RECENT TIMES

PLAYERS GONE

Rumors were that Will Bynum wasn't going to return for his sophomore year. Bynum denied them.

The rumors were later fueled when midway through UA's trip to Australia, Bynum returned to the states to be with his sick mom.

"You just knew he didn't want to be there," said Ryan Hansen. "Then he found out about Michael Dickerson and his excuse about his grandmother being ill."

So Bynum returned home, fueling more speculation that his days with Arizona were numbered.

But Bynum came back to UA for his sophomore season.

"We never thought we'd see him again," said Hansen. "He was jovial and was ready to fit in."

And he played plenty early in the season, filling in for an injured Salim Stoudamire and an injured Luke Walton. And at times he shined, starting in two games and playing in eight. He averaged 7.8 points a game. But then Stoudamire got healthy as did Walton, making him a fixture on the bench. Arizona still needed him for depth, however.

"But he got disgruntled and was gone," Hansen said.

He did it oddly. He didn't go to UA's practice the day the team left for Oregon, telling a teammate that he'd make the team flight. He never did. In a later interview, while he was with Georgia Tech, he said he had "been hypnotized by Arizona."

Two months later, Dennis Latimore called it quits at Arizona. No one knew why, but he just decided to leave. Was it playing time? Was it just unhappiness?

It came just a couple of weeks after UA had gone to Kansas, giving him a trip home to see friends. Days later, Latimore decided to leave the program.

"We all called him on his cell phone and no one knew where he was," said Hansen. "No one heard anything. He was gone. He never came back."

Latimore, a smart, studious guy, stayed in school, later deciding he'd attend Notre Dame.

"No question he was a smart, articulate, quiet guy," Hansen said. "He'd read poetry. He'd read Homer for fun. He enjoyed reading. You could tell that basketball was not a priority.

"I guess he didn't feel he could talk to anyone, yet he was as articulate as anyone we've had here.

"He just didn't have anyone to talk to."

CANDYGATE

Arizona was about to play in perhaps the biggest nonconference game of the season, traveling to Lawrence, Kansas, for a huge matchup between the Jayhawks and the Wildcats.

Arizona won the game, running away for a 91-74 win. But that wasn't the story that drew the most buzz. The next day news broke that a witness saw a couple of Arizona players taking snack-food merchandise from a vending machine the morning of the noon game against KU.

The total value of the merchandise was about $80. In haste to catch a plane, Arizona coaches said they'd pay what was said was owed.

The witness said the two players he recognized were senior Luke Walton and sophomore Salim Stoudamire, although the witness later said it may not have been Stoudamire.

The witness never spoke to the media, instead hiring an attorney. That same week, Olson called the "witness" a "yahoo," asking how you could trust a witness who had Kansas ties. The witness was a Kansas grad. From that point on until the end of the season, the team got grief for the alleged incident.

"It was frustrating because I know I didn't do anything, but just because some random guy says something, I'm named," said Walton. "They just threw my name out there, and everyone assumed I was part of it."

Arizona, attempting to become the first team to go undefeated in conference play, lost its next game, falling to 82-77 for its lone loss in conference.

Olson blamed the loss on all the commotion Candygate caused.

"I talked to every one of our players and all the people back there," UA's Jim Livengood said. "I think there could be some culpability on both sides. Did we break into a candy machine? I don't think so. Was a candy machine open? I think so. Go from there."

Point-forward Luke Walton could do it all, making him one of the most versatile players in the history of Arizona basketball. (Stephen Dunn/Getty Images)

LOST JERSEY

It was a disaster waiting to happen on March 13, 2003. Conference champion Arizona didn't really want to be at the Pac-10 Conference tournament. It already had a No. 1 seed in the West locked up for the NCAA tournament, which was scheduled a week later. But Arizona played anyway.

It did have its problems nonetheless. While getting ready for the game—an afternoon contest—team managers realized they forgot to pack Gardner's jersey top, No. 22.

What to do? Arizona had little time. The last thing Gardner wanted to do was wear someone else's number.

So they called UA and had equipment manager Tim Pfennig get the uniform and jump on a flight from Tucson to Los Angeles.

"We came in at about the 11-minute mark and Tim handed it to me after taking a taxi from LAX to Staples Center," said Ryan Hansen. "I met him at the top of the ramp and ran to the locker room. At the 10-minute mark I handed Jason the jersey."

Hansen said it was pure mayhem and a very stressful time.

"I was going to wear No. 12, the number of my good friend, Phil Torres," Gardner said. "I'd worn No. 22 since I was a kid. I warmed up in a white (tank-top t-shirt) under my warmups and felt naked as I don't know what."

He played one of his worst games of the season, going two for 20 from the floor in the upset loss, 96-89, to UCLA.

IT'S WAR

It happened in 1991 with the war in Kuwait and again in 2003 when the USA went to war in Afghanistan. In 2003, Arizona was about to play in the first round of the NCAA tournament when talk started about the well-being of soldiers and their families. Basketball was secondary.

"It was really hard to stay focused, knowing that you had U.S. citizens and people close to you going to war," said UA's Chris Rodgers. "It was a difficult time for the country."

Arizona players also reflected on the fact many of those going to war were their ages—18, 19, 20.

"That's what makes you grateful to have the opportunity you have," he said. "I'm getting to do something I enjoy. It's not so serious where it's life threatening. It makes me appreciate all the things I do have.

"It was just a tough time."

No Doom and Gloom II

Two seasons after the trio of Wright, Jefferson and Arenas left early for the NBA, Arizona and Olson found themselves in a different yet similar situation. Highly touted recruit Ndudi Ebi, rated as the second best high school player behind LeBron James, committed and signed with Arizona in November, saying the NBA would have to wait because he wanted to go to Arizona. There was, however, a caveat—the NBA was still an option.

Seven months later Ebi, a lanky six-foot-nine, 195-pound forward, declared for the NBA, deciding to keep his name in the draft.

It came a day after he told Olson in a telephone conversation he still intended on attending UA.

"We had no idea this was going to happen," Olson said. "It's a first."

Adding, "It's disappointing, but the program will go on. We'll be good without him, but we would have been better with him."

It has changed the way Olson recruits. He said had he known there was even a remote chance Ebi was going to go pro he likely would not have recruited him so hard—if at all. And Olson had spent a lot of time on Ebi, who was also being recruited by Duke and Texas.

AND THE WINNER IS...

It's a rare occurrence when the NCAA men's basketball Tournament committee chairman is the one who hands over the national championship trophy to his coach. But that seemed to be the theme for most of the 2002-2003 season when Jim Livengood was the NCAA Tournament chairman.

With Arizona considered to be the best team in the country for parts of the season behind seniors Walton and Gardner, Livengood was asked a number of times how he'd feel about being only the second person to hand the trophy to his coach. Back in 1998, then-chairman C.M. Newton, then the AD at Kentucky, handed the trophy over to Tubby Smith.

Livengood never got the chance. UA lost to Kansas, 78-75, in the West Region finals.

"It was when I allowed myself to be selfish," Livengood said, of being disappointed. "I rationalize it because I would have been proud of our team and so proud of Lute."

Livengood's duties went on, however, as he congratulated Syracuse coach Jim Boeheim for winning the title.

"As I stood there on Monday night (the night of the title) I thought, 'Man, this could have been Lute,'" Livengood said. "It would have been a thrill."

It looked like a good possibility at points throughout the Kansas game. Livengood said he and Tom Jernstedt, the NCAA's deputy executive director, were watching the game after seeing Marquette upset Kentucky in another regional when Tom turned to him to say it appeared Arizona would make it after making a late-game run to close the gap to three.

"They will be there," Jernstedt said. "They were going to New Orleans."

It never happened.

SIMON, ANOTHER PLAYER

While attempting to rehab his injured left knee, Miles Simon returned to Arizona, attending school to get his degree. Five months after his surgery, Simon helped UA in practices, often times playing the opponent's best player on the scout team. At times he was Oregon's Luke Jackson or Washington's Brandon Roy or Washington State's Marcus Moore.

Who would have thought that seven years after being named Arizona's MVP at the 1997 Final Four Simon would be helping on the scout team? Not him. He was rarely a scout-team player when he was a regular player.

"I probably would have thought you were crazy," he said, of any thought of being a scout team player at age 28. "It's fun. Coach O is giving me a good chance to get back into shape, play and get my feel back for the game. I'm thankful for the opportunity."

UA players liked it.

"He knows the system and he's a great player," Hassan Adams said. "He's smart."

CURSES—WELL, NOT EXACTLY

Olson never curses. But during the 2003-04 season, he might have.

At one point in a practice, Arizona players—Andre Iguodala specifically—were complaining about practice.

"We were arguing and the team was going at each other," Iguodala said. "We were complaining about fouls and things. He was pretty ticked. He let us know by cursing. It was different."

It's still debatable if Olson actually did.

What Olson said was, "bitch, bitch, bitch," referring to the players and all they did was complain.

"It was funny at the time, but we also knew he was trying to get his point across," Iguodala said. "We didn't take it as a cuss word, but he said it, so we laughed."

GIVING THE FINGER

Arizona's rivalry with Arizona State had long been a one-sided affair since Olson arrived at Arizona in 1983. In fact, UA, behind Olson, was 36-5 against Arizona State going into the 2003-2004 season.

It was win No. 37, which proved to be one that got ASU coach Rob Evans steamed and Olson criticized. The criticism came from Evans, after he saw Olson point to the scoreboard after—and before—ASU students began chanting obscene things to the Hall of Fame coach.

Olson just wanted the students to know that his team had a 91-65 lead late in the game. Moments earlier he had been given a technical for getting on the refs.

Then the chants came, "Lute's an asshole. Lute's an asshole."

Olson then pointed to the scoreboard—again.

"I've put up with learning all kinds of new words from that student section over the years, and thought that probably you should learn to keep your mouth closed when you are down 30-something points," Olson said. "I've been called every name that you can be called, and I think it's frankly disgusting. They deserved that and more.

"It's 21 years of listening to it, so I thought that probably it's time that they got a response. In the past I've always ignored it, but I think that there's a time when you should just keep your mouth shut and enjoy the rest of the game. That didn't keep them hushed. In fact, I got more. But at least I felt better."

Olson's players and coaches got a kick out of it. To the players and his assistants, it showed the usually stoic, straight-laced Olson had a sense of humor, that he could show a side he normally didn't show.

Two days later, Evans reacted, telling the *Arizona Republic* that Olson's actions were "a classless act."

Olson declined comment on the incident, later saying it was one man's opinion.

Perhaps that's what the rivalry needed—some finger waving and some fodder from the coaches.

Not lost in that game was the fact that Olson became the 19th coach in college basketball history to reach the 700-win mark.

"It just means I've been around a long time," he said.

Chapter 13

LUTE OLSON

HE'S GONE

On two occasions Olson had a chance to leave to coach the University of Kentucky. The first time was in 1985 when Joe B. Hall retired, and another time in 1989 when Eddie Sutton resigned under fire after a scandal involving players.

In 1985, Olson wasn't initially interested, but after a newspaper report erroneously reported Olson had a conflict of interest in the purchase of team uniforms, Olson felt his integrity had been called into question and thought Kentucky might be the place to be.

He and Bobbi visited Lexington, and after interviews for a day, the Olsons returned home. He had decided Kentucky wasn't the place for him. He felt they blew the interview process in part because they failed to include Bobbi, his wife of more than 30 years, in any of the discussions.

"They never did talk to Bobbi," Olson said. "They never showed her the campus or Rupp Arena. That was a big mistake on their part. We had always been a team."

Kentucky officials knew they erred after the Olsons turned them down. A day later, Kentucky officials called back, admitting their error, but the Olsons had already decided they were going to stay in Tucson.

"I was concerned, but once I found out how they were recruiting him, I felt comfortable he wasn't going to go," said Cedric Dempsey, then the UA athletic director. "Having gone through the hiring experience with him, I knew Bobbi was a very important part of his life and the process. More people may have been more concerned than I was."

But by the time Olson returned to Tucson, he had made up his mind Arizona was the place to be after receiving countless letters and support to stay.

"I thought he was gone," said Scott Thompson, an assistant at UA at the time. "But he said he was staying at Arizona. We'll have to win a national championship."

Four years later, Kentucky called again. This time Kentucky was no match for the Olsons.

"I guess the turning point was when my wife picked up two grandkids from school that day, and on the way home they said something to her about that's OK if you and Papa Lute decide to go," Olson said. "While they are saying that they've got tears streaming down their faces. Those who are grandparents, you'll understand how that tugs at you."

Olson called C.M. Newton, Kentucky's then-AD, to tell him he wasn't going to make the trip for a visit.

"Family has always been critical to us," Olson said. "That was why we decided that Arizona would be a good place for us to finish things up."

Again, Dempsey didn't feel Olson would leave.

"I never thought he'd go at that point," he said. "I wasn't convinced that all the things and reasons he didn't go the first time had changed."

THE PHILOSOPHY

It's been long said and written that Olson is a disciple of former UCLA great and legendary coach John Wooden. As a high school coach in Southern California in the mid-1960s, Olson worked a number of Wooden basketball camps.

It was then—early in his basketball coaching days—when Olson developed the philosophy that games are won in practices.

"Our philosophy is very simple, and it's about every day a player comes out here and should leave the court a better player," Olson said. "And that's coming from an individual standpoint and from helping the team."

It's a reason why Olson doesn't usually place his best five players on the court as a unit, going against the second five. He often mixes and matches lineups in scrimmages and in practices to get the best competition going.

"People were shocked Jason Terry would go from being a reserve to an All-American in just a year," Olson said. "Part of it was that even though he was a reserve, he played point guard every minute in practice when he was going up against Mike Bibby."

Most recently, it was Simon going against Dickerson; Arenas going against Jefferson; Walton vs. Iguodala.

"It's very important in the development because they know they can't take a day off of practice," Olson said. "If they do, they'll come out and get embarrassed. We've long looked at it like the day of the game is like a day off compared to what you see in practice. You learn the game in practice, and you display what you've learned in the game."

The Criticism

It wasn't a good feeling in the early to mid-1990s in the basketball program. Stunning first-round losses were more the norm than the exception.

Figure that in 1992, Arizona, a No. 3 seed in the Southeast, was a heavy favorite over 14-seed East Tennessee State. Arizona lost, 87–80.

A season later, Arizona became just the second No. 2 seed to lose to a No. 15 seed (Santa Clara) in the NCAAs.

What it all meant was just a decade after Olson had arrived—and built a thriving and growing power in the West—some people were publicly wondering if Olson was the man to take the team to the next level. This just five years after taking the Wildcats to their first Final Four.

Olson's response at the time?

"There's a saying, 'The best talker and the worst flyer among the birds is the parrot.' I relate that a little to fans. The ones that are most involved, most supportive of the program, are the ones you can really count on," Olson said. "The ones that create 90-plus percent of the criticism are the ones who don't really understand what's being done."

A year later, Olson was back in the Final Four for the second time. Three years later, UA, behind Olson, was winning its first NCAA title.

New love

They met at the 2002 Final Four in Atlanta, Lute Olson and Christine Toretti. The pairing was set up through June Dempsey, the wife of former UA athletic director Cedric Dempsey.

The two spoke over dinner at an NCAA function and hit it off. They spoke for hours via phone, later developing a romance that seemed like destiny. There was a problem, however. She lived in Pennsylvania; he in Tucson.

Meetings would be brief and encounters minimal, after all, Olson was going to be in the middle of a season where his team was considered the best in the country.

Then the romance became more serious. Toretti started to show up at games, yet they kept it a secret.

"I went to the LSU game (in December) and sat with someone not associated with UA," Toretti said. "Then I went to the Fiesta Bowl Classic (in Tucson) and no one seemed to notice."

Then she went to the Kansas game in January.

People started to wonder who she was. They'd been seen here and there, but there she had no connection to UA.

"I just said I was here to support Lute," she said, showing the same coyness she gave them.

Then things got serious. After UA beat Kansas, Olson proposed marriage.

It stayed quiet for about one and a half months before news broke that Olson was headed to the altar.

While preparing for the wedding, someone close to her family leaked the news to a Pittsburgh-area society-page editor.

"I called Lute to say that I was sorry but they planned on running something about it," Toretti said. "But the good news was it was going to run in the gossip section of the paper and no one would read it. ... I had no idea of Lute's popularity."

That day, news organizations in Tucson wanted to know if the news was true.

"Lydia (Olson's secretary) came down to the court and she never does that, but she said that people were calling to know if the news was true," Olson said.

He declined comment on all accounts, deciding to speak on the matter the next day.

About 25 people made the press conference with the main topic of conversation being: was he planning on retiring? Hardly, he said, he loved what he did and who he was doing it for.

"We had hoped to keep it quiet until the end of the season so it wouldn't be a distraction, but when it did come out, it wasn't one," Olson said.

Arizona already had clinched the Pac-10 regular season title and was getting ready for its final two regular-season games, conference tournament and the NCAA Tournament.

HE'S PROFESSIONAL

It's often been said Olson runs his program like a CEO would a Fortune 500 company. And yes, he's the CEO. He also has that presence. He has a regal and towering presence and a grandfatherly look.

"When you come to school you think you're going to hang out there in his office," Bruce Fraser said. "When you step on campus you realize that's not the case. You realize you're in a business now. I think he'd like to get closer to his players, but that's how he is. That's how he keeps and maintains his respect."

It's one of the reasons why Arizona has been one of the more successful programs in the country over the past two decades. It's treated like a business.

"He's a professional coach," Blair said, of UA coach Lute Olson. "And by professional I mean he treats it like a professional team. Coach Olson isn't going to come and walk you to class. You're the one who has to do that, but when you step in between those lines you're his. That's just the way it is. He

Hall of Fame coach Lute Olson treats his teams with a businesslike attitude—just get it done.

treats you like a grown man. Other teams have curfews, but we didn't. He trusts you to be professional.

"He's a guy you learn from because of his professionalism. It could cause problems for some. It takes a while to learn, but you have to."

IT'S COACH OLSON

Blair has long been known to be a person who speaks his mind, even if it means upsetting someone. Throughout his career at UA, he'd occasionally throw in an expletive or two during an interview. At one point in his junior season, Blair refused to talk to the media because it got back to him he may be cursing a bit too much. His thought was: "If I can't say what I want to say, I won't say it at all."

His embargo on the press lasted a week.

He did get in a bit of trouble when Olson read in a story where Blair referred to him as Lute.

"He said, 'Joe whenever you do interviews, call me Coach O or Coach Olson and not Lute,'" Blair said. "That was the only time he ever said anything to me about interviews. And that's surprising, because I go back and read some of the interviews I've done and I'm surprised I said it.

"I think Coach Olson respected what I had to say and that I spoke my mind.

"I never spoke anything detrimental about the team. I spoke my mind and still do."

NIX THE SOLO ACT

In Olson's time as coach, there have been 17 transfers in the program. More recently, there have been seven in the last five years. Mostly, it's all about playing time. The players want it, and either they are not ready to get significant minutes or there is a logjam at the position.

"Once you make yourself useful to the program, you'll get minutes in the game," said Corey Williams. "That's the biggest thing guys coming into the program have to understand. If you show that you can do it, it will be acknowledged and you'll get thrown into the mix.

"But the solo act will never fly at Arizona. There are transfers here every year because they can't grasp that concept. Doing your own thing doesn't necessarily mean success."

ONE ERA TO ANOTHER

Every now and again former UA players visit McKale Center or Arizona's basketball office. It happens more often nowadays. It doesn't matter what era, but more specifically those in Olson's era visit all the time.

"I was in there one day and we had me, Damon Stoudamire, Channing Frye and Hassan Adams in there talking," Miles Simon said. "Dudes were 19 years old to 30 years old. Everybody gets along so well. It's a special place. Young guys appreciate what the older guys did, and the older guys still watch the younger guys and what they do."

Mr. Stoic

If there's one thing that has remained constant throughout Olson's coaching career it's been his demeanor on the court. He's fiery on it and as cool as they come after the game.

Consider when he was the head coach of the United States National team in 1986 and it pulled off a shocker in beating USSR, 87-85, to win the gold medal at the 1986 World Basketball Championships, the last amateur team to win a gold medal at that level.

"I can remember Lute, with that confident look, going to shake the hand of the Soviet coach and looking as though he had just won another basketball game," said then UA and World Championship assistant Scott Thompson. "He wasn't jumping around and hugging people. It was real funny, and he had just won the World Championship."

But as Thompson knows it's not about getting excited … at least not in public.

"My philosophy has always been that if the kids are going to maintain their poise and composure on the court, then they shouldn't see a raving maniac on the sidelines," Olson said. "On the other hand, if they get used to seeing that, it probably isn't a distraction to them."

Such was the case in an epic game against Gonzaga during the 2003 NCAA Tournament. Gonzaga gave UA fits for a game and two overtimes before the Wildcats prevailed in unbelievable to-and-fro game.

"Like I've said, what shows on the exterior doesn't necessarily show what's going on inside," Olson said.

RECORD BREAKER

It was quite an accomplishment when Olson won his 510th game while Arizona's coach. It meant he became the school's all-time winningest coach, surpassing the late Fred A. Enke, who finished with 509 in 36 years of coaching.

Arizona's 97-72 rout of UCLA was the game that did it.

"It comes at a memorable place," said Olson of Pauley Pavilion.

But that's all he'd say when it came to getting the record. Others, however, had thoughts.

"Lute Olson just amazes me," said Dick Vitale. "He's getting better and better like good wine. The bottom line is that he has a great grasp for winning. He knows what the team concept is all about. That's why he is a genuine, solid-gold Hall of Famer. All the numbers he's putting up are great. He looks younger and younger. And his program is better than it has ever been."

Former UA coach Bruce Larson never thought the number—509—would be surpassed.

"That's such a big number," said Larson, who succeeded Enke in 1961. "Fred was here so long. But what Lute has done is unbelievable."

Former USC coach George Raveling agreed.

"I'm at a point now where nothing Lute does surprises me anymore," said Raveling, who also coached at Washington State and succeeded Olson at Iowa in 1983. "Anything he does adds to the legacy. It'll put enormous pressure on anyone who comes after him. I'd hate to be the guy who follows him."

Enke Jr., said, "Records are to be broken. Lute has done an excellent job."

So good that Arizona went from a horrible 4-24 record in 1983 to one of the top-five men's basketball programs under Olson.

"The program was in such bad shape that I didn't get the impression that he was looking that far into the future to think he'd be in Tucson for 21 years," said Thompson. "At that stage, the program was just trying to improve little by little, week by week. It's very rare to see coaches stay at one place for that long."

In that span, Olson has averaged just under 25 wins a season.

"Who would have dreamt that?" Thompson said. "That's an amazing thing."

Lute Roasted

Olson looked very uncomfortable the night he was publicly roasted. He cringed most of the night, reacting to a number of jokes and barbs aimed at him from the likes of Kerr, Tolbert and O'Neill among others at the Lute Olson Dinner/Roast.

"All you hear about him is this and that, a mother-approved coach. It's true. But we all know he'd like to be me for a day," said O'Neill, the former fiery UA assistant and recent Toronto Raptors head coach. "I'd like to be you (Olson) for a day, so I can clean out your damn bank account and get the hell out of town."

Friend and former Arizona State coach Bill Frieder said it was appropriate he was asked to roast because, "I'm the one who made this guy very famous with the Bank One commercials."

He added it was hard to come up with nice things to say, but after speaking to someone he found out that Olson was "arrogant, aloof and egotistical."

"But I know him well enough to say that's not true," Frieder said. "It's exactly the opposite, he's egotistical, then aloof, then arrogant."

Former players Kerr and Elliott said it was difficult to come up with anything bad to say about their former coach, but it wasn't so difficult for former player Tolbert, a constant thorn in Olson's side the two years Tolbert was in a Wildcat uniform.

"What's the one thing people always talk about? The hair," Tolbert said, as he placed a hand on the perfect coif. "I just won five bucks because one of my friends said it was hair club for men. There is no way (it is). But it does look like mountain goat hair up there."

Celebrate the Heroes of College Basketball
in These Other 2004 Releases from Sports Publishing!